INTRODUCTION

Ukulele Fretboard Atlas is a collection of roadmaps for the most important scales and chords (up to seventh chords). The material is presented in all 12 keys, using 12-fret neck diagrams with color-coded displays of the most common moveable fingerings. When fingerings share common notes, the colors will overlap. No music reading or understanding of music theory is required.

Mastering the ukulele neck can be challenging, even for very experienced players. There are several obstacles that make learning the ukulele's fretboard difficult. On the ukulele, a note can be played in several different places, unlike many other instruments, where each note has only one location. Additionally, the ukulele's fourth string (G) is commonly tuned higher than the third and second strings (C and E, respectively), making it slightly tricky to get used to at first if you're coming to the instrument from a guitar background.

The diagrams in *Ukulele Fretboard Atlas* will help you quickly internalize and memorize not only the most common scales and chords, but also others that may have previously seemed impossible to grasp. You'll be able to easily see and understand how scale and chord shapes are laid out, and how they connect and overlap across the neck. As an added benefit, once you can see a shape in your mind's eye, you've got all 12 keys covered—just move the shape to start on a different fret, depending on the key you want.

ABOUT THE AUTHOR

New York City native Joe Charupakorn is a guitarist, editor, and best-selling author. He has written over 25 instructional books for Hal Leonard Corporation. His books are available worldwide and have been translated into many languages.

Visit him on the web at *joecharupakorn.com*.

HOW TO USE THIS BOOK

A good plan of attack with *Ukulele Fretboard Atlas* would be to start by learning the most common scales, which are the major, natural minor (Aeolian), minor pentatonic, major pentatonic, and blues scales. After getting comfortable with these (or if the need arises), then add in some of the more complex scales and modes presented in this book.

First, start with one scale shape and work with it for a while in one key until it feels comfortable. When you've internalized that one shape, add in an adjacent shape in the same key. Once you can see both shapes independently and also as pieces of a bigger puzzle, then practice going back and forth between the two. Eventually add in more fingerings in the same key, and before long, you'll have the whole neck covered. There are countless ways to put the scale shapes to use. For example, you can run the scales straight up and down, improvise with them, or sight-read, using the shapes as a reference. Do this in all 12 keys.

For the chord section, start with power chords and triads, which are the backbone of virtually any style of music and fall into the "must-know" category. After you have got a firm grasp on these chords, learn the triads with added notes and seventh chords to add harmonic color to your music. To internalize chord shapes, first take some time to get a mental picture of the chord's shape. After committing it to memory, practice getting to the shape quickly without referring to the book and also make sure all the notes are ringing clearly. Then add another voicing of the same chord and practice moving back and forth between the two voicings. Once you are comfortable with this, do it in the remaining keys. To gain flexibility with the new chords, practice a short progression of two or three chords in different keys, at first using two voicings for each chord. Then add more voicings as it becomes second nature. Also try creating solo arrangements of some of your favorite tunes and put these new shapes to use.

Beyond the Fingering

For each diagram, every tone of the specific scale or chord is circled, but only the most common moveable shapes are displayed with color codes. Note that, because the ukulele's fourth string isn't often used outside of chordal playing, the scale fingerings in this book are only color-coded from the third to the first strings. Of course, all the notes of every scale—including the ones on the fourth string—are circled, so if you want to experiment with using notes on the fourth string melodically, by all means, feel free to explore.

The fingerings presented are just a starting point—you shouldn't feel "locked in" to any of the shapes presented. You can take fragments from one fingering and combine it with fragments from an adjacent fingering to create your own shapes that might be more suitable for a specific situation. Use the circled scale and chord tones as a guide and go for it! Because they all interconnect, the idea is that, ultimately, you'll see the ukulele neck as one unit.

UKULELE FRETBOARD ATLAS

GET A BETTER GRIP ON NECK NAVIGATION!

BY JOE CHARUPAKORN

ISBN 978-1-4950-8037-1

HAL•LEONARD®

7777 W. BLUEMOUND RD. P.O. BOX 13819 MILWAUKEE, WI 53213

In Australia Contact:
Hal Leonard Australia Pty. Ltd.
4 Lentara Court
Cheltenham, Victoria, 3192 Australia
Email: ausadmin@halleonard.com.au

Visit Hal Leonard Online at
www.halleonard.com

TABLE OF CONTENTS

NOTATION CONVENTIONS IN THIS BOOK

Any note with an *accidental*—a sharp or flat—can be spelled either as a sharp or flat version of the note. In this book, both the sharp and flat versions of every note (*enharmonic equivalents*) are displayed on the fretboard diagrams. The specific accidentals used in the "proper" spelling of a scale or chord will generally depend on the context.

For example, here is the proper spelling of the G major scale:

G A B C D E F♯ G

And here is an incorrect spelling of the G major scale:

G A B C D E G♭ G

F♯ is the same note as G♭, and, in our diagrams, any note location with that pitch is represented by F♯/G♭ on the fretboard. However, the correct spelling of the G major scale is the one with F♯ because this spelling lets us represent every letter in the music alphabet. In the spelling with G♭, there are no Fs of any kind and two kinds of Gs—a G♭ and a G.

In the headings above the diagrams throughout the book, only the most commonly accepted spellings of the specific scales or chords are displayed.

Exceptions to the Rule

In some cases, it's more practical to suspend the rigidity of the rules and go with a more familiar, if technically "wrong," spelling. This is particularly common in cases involving scales and chords that have double sharps (𝄪) and double flats (𝄫) in their proper spelling.

The fretboard diagrams in *Ukulele Fretboard Atlas* do not include double sharps (𝄪) or double flats (𝄫), or less common accidentals such as F♭, C♭, etc. However, the proper spellings of scales and chords are listed in the headings above the diagrams throughout the book.

For example, the proper spelling of A♭ melodic minor is:

A♭ B♭ C♭ D♭ E♭ F G

While C♭ is enharmonically the same note as B, the dots representing the C♭ notes will be on the fretboard diagram's B notes.

If this is all a little confusing, the good news is that, even without any of this information, you'll be able to play any of the scales or chords in any key as long as you can follow the diagrams.

SCALES

THE MAJOR SCALE
AND ITS MODES

C IONIAN

C–D–E–F–G–A–B

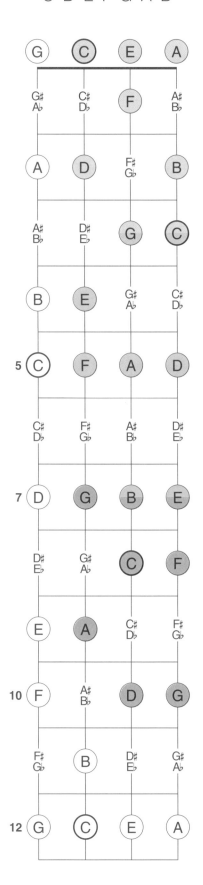

C#/Db IONIAN

C#–D#–E#–F#–G#–A#–B#
Db–Eb–F–Gb–Ab–Bb–C

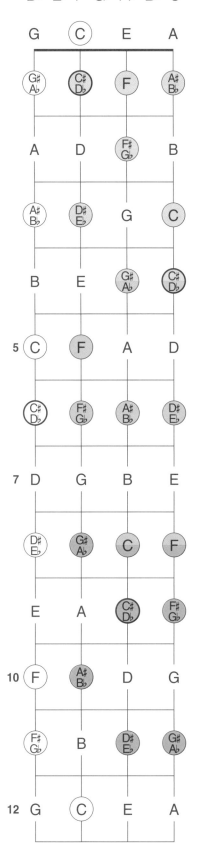

D IONIAN

D–E–F#–G–A–B–C#

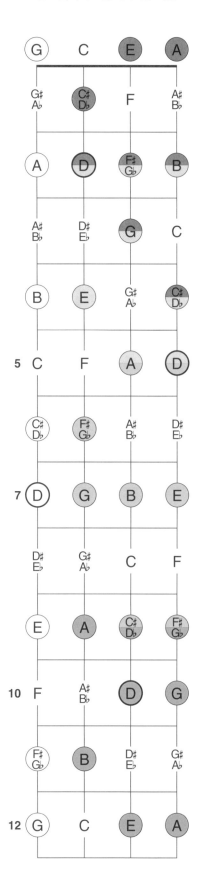

E♭ IONIAN

E♭–F–G–A♭–B♭–C–D

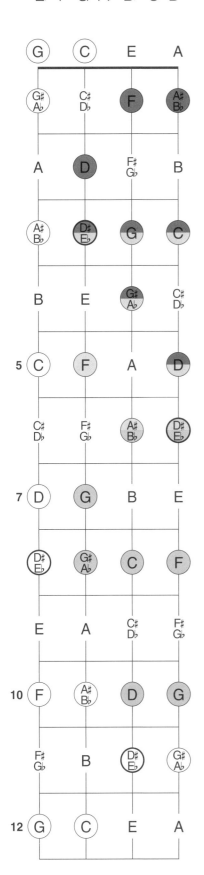

E IONIAN

E–F♯–G♯–A–B–C♯–D♯

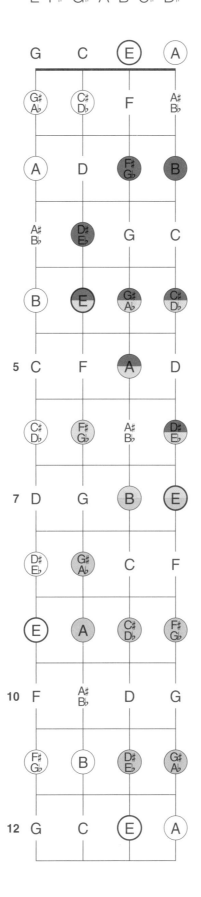

F IONIAN

F–G–A–B♭–C–D–E

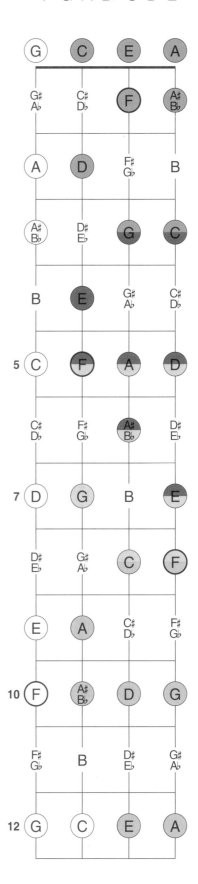

9

F#/Gb IONIAN

F#–G#–A#–B–C#–D#–E#
Gb–Ab–Bb–Cb–Db–Eb–F

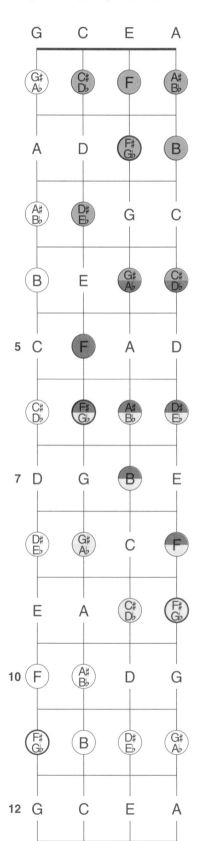

G IONIAN

G–A–B–C–D–E–F#

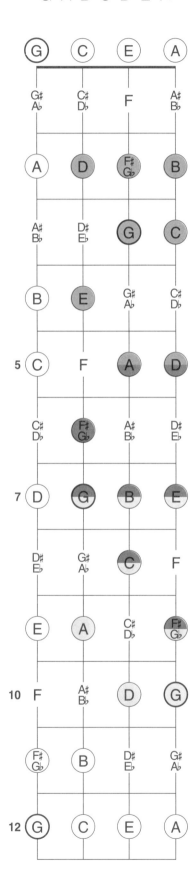

Ab IONIAN

Ab–Bb–C–Db–Eb–F–G

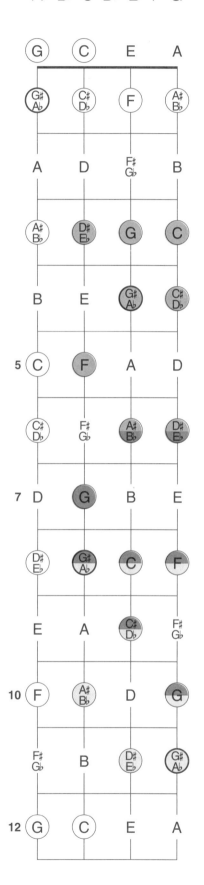

A IONIAN

A–B–C#–D–E–F#–G#

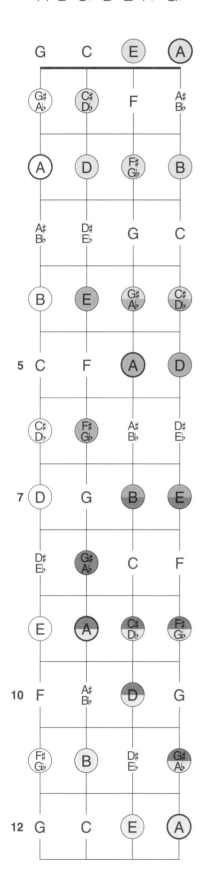

Bb IONIAN

Bb–C–D–Eb–F–G–A

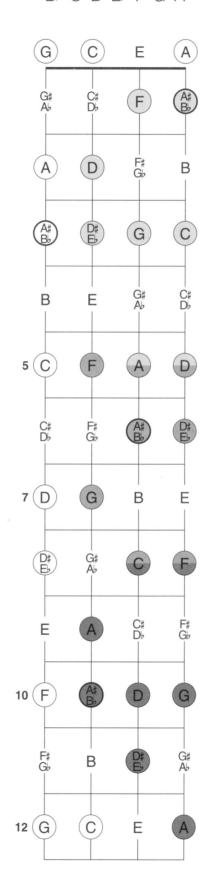

B IONIAN

B–C#–D#–E–F#–G#–A#

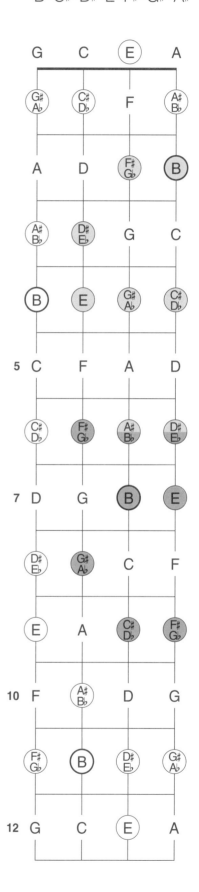

11

C DORIAN

C–D–E♭–F–G–A–B♭

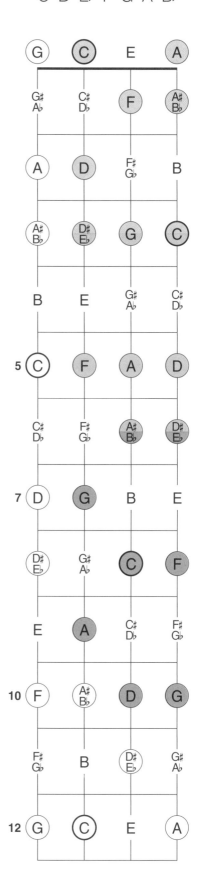

C♯ DORIAN

C♯–D♯–E–F♯–G♯–A♯–B

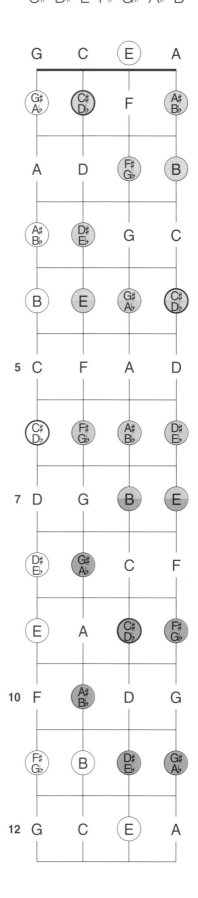

D DORIAN

D–E–F–G–A–B–C

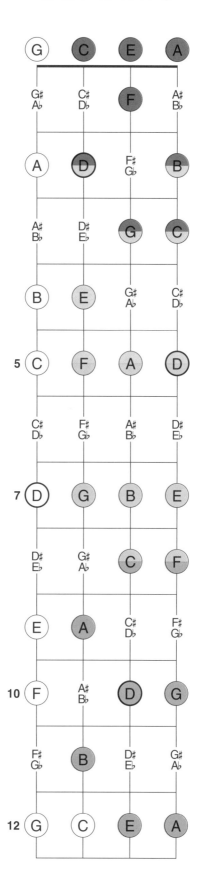

E♭ DORIAN

E♭–F–G♭–A♭–B♭–C–D♭

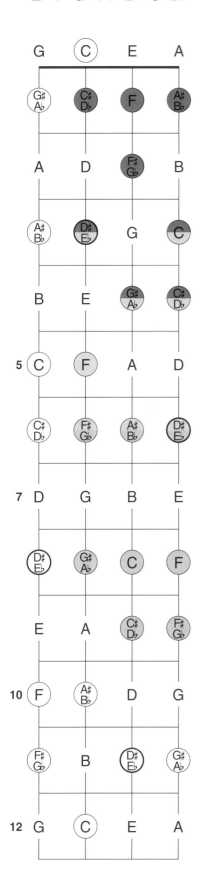

E DORIAN

E–F♯–G–A–B–C♯–D

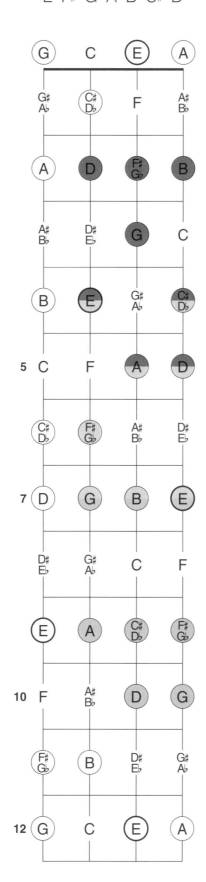

F DORIAN

F–G–A♭–B♭–C–D–E♭

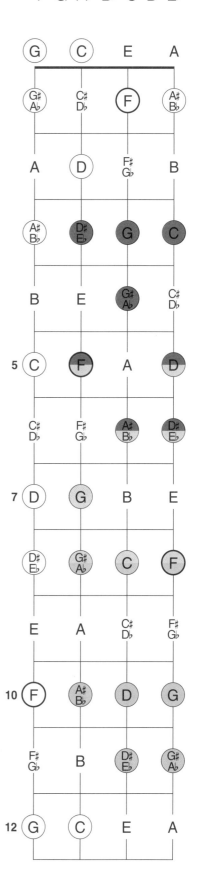

F# DORIAN

F#–G#–A–B–C#–D#–E

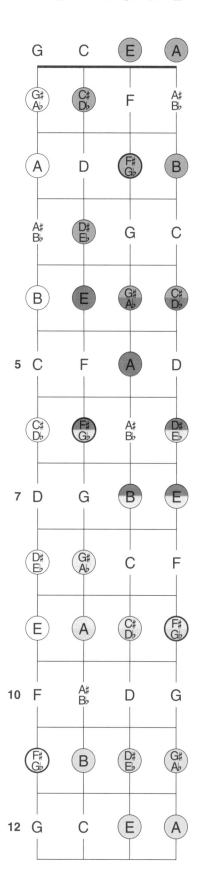

G DORIAN

G–A–B♭–C–D–E–F

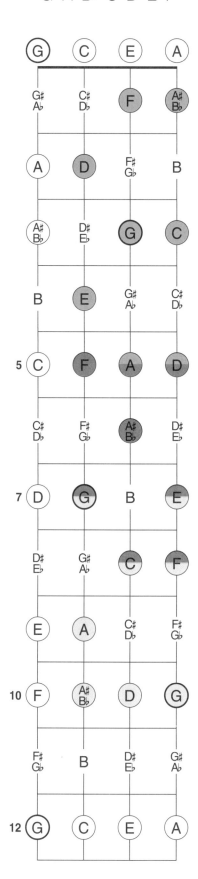

A♭ DORIAN

A♭–B♭–C♭–D♭–E♭–F–G♭

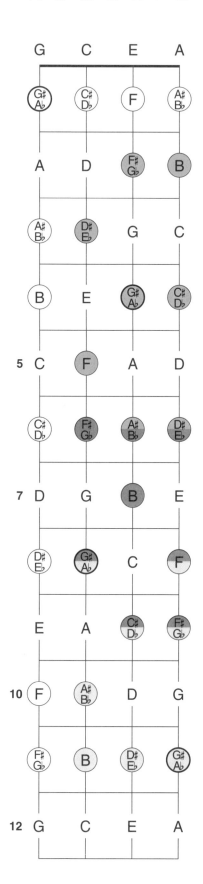

A DORIAN

A–B–C–D–E–F#–G

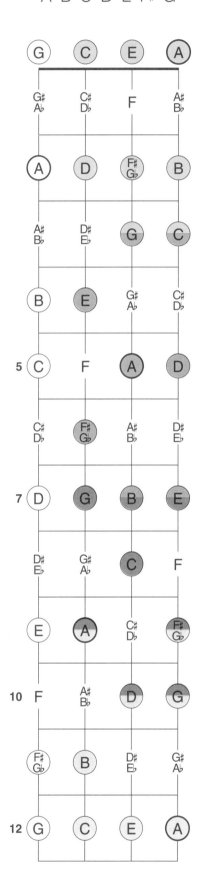

Bb DORIAN

Bb–C–Db–Eb–F–G–Ab

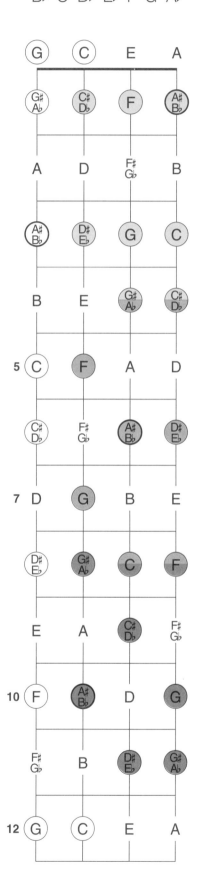

B DORIAN

B–C#–D–E–F#–G#–A

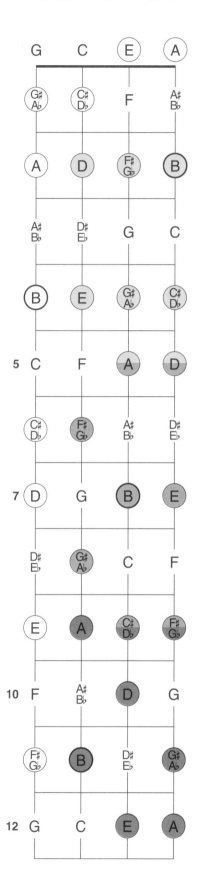

C PHRYGIAN

C–Db–Eb–F–G–Ab–Bb

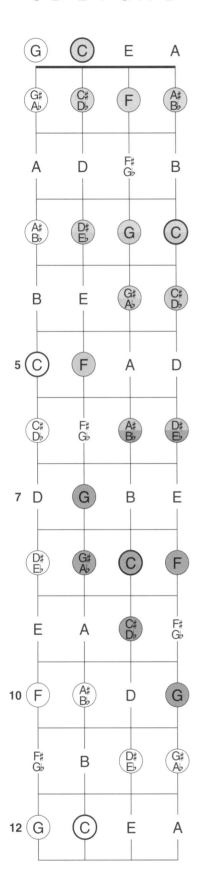

C# PHRYGIAN

C#–D–E–F#–G#–A–B

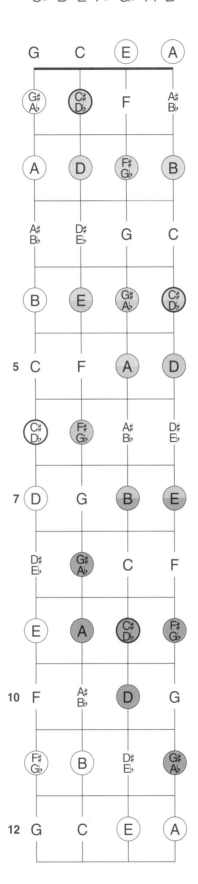

D PHRYGIAN

D–Eb–F–G–A–Bb–C

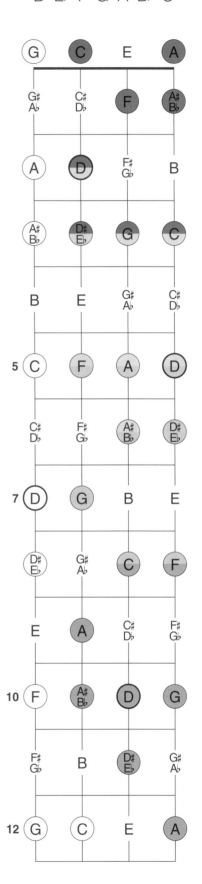

D♯ PHRYGIAN

D♯–E–F♯–G♯–A♯–B–C♯

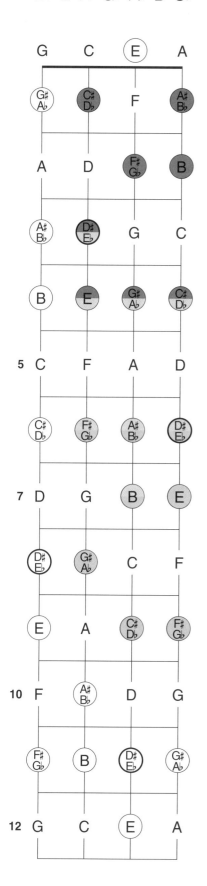

E PHRYGIAN

E–F–G–A–B–C–D

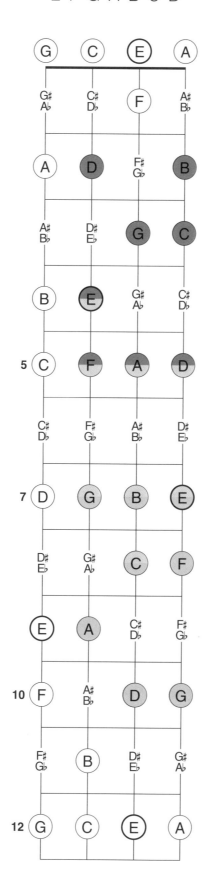

F PHRYGIAN

F–G♭–A♭–B♭–C–D♭–E♭

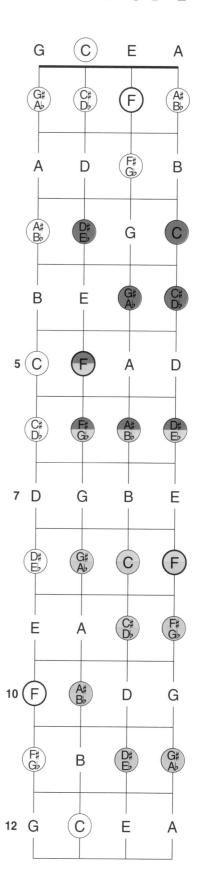

F# PHRYGIAN

F#–G–A–B–C#–D–E

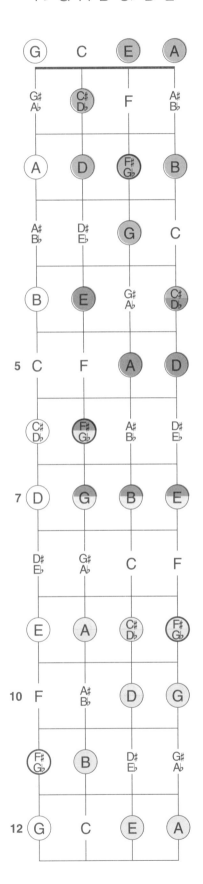

G PHRYGIAN

G–A♭–B♭–C–D–E♭–F

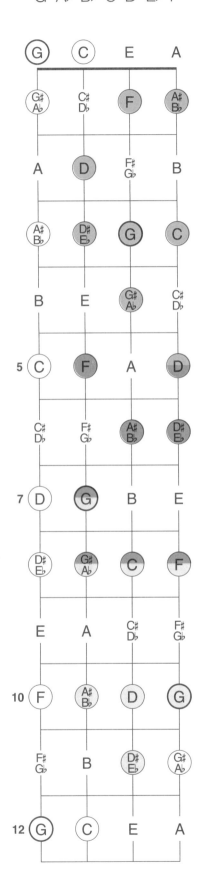

G# PHRYGIAN

G#–A–B–C#–D#–E–F#

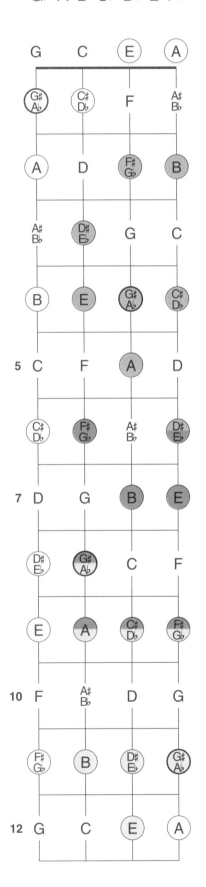

A PHRYGIAN

A–B♭–C–D–E–F–G

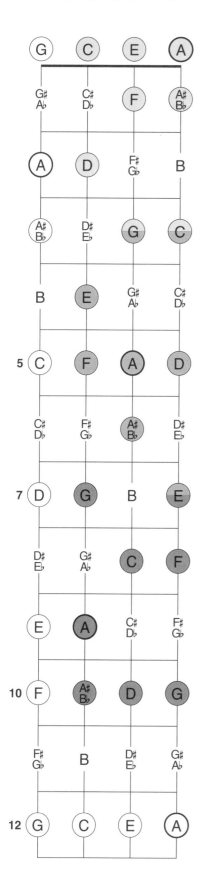

B♭ PHRYGIAN

B♭–C♭–D♭–E♭–F–G♭–A♭

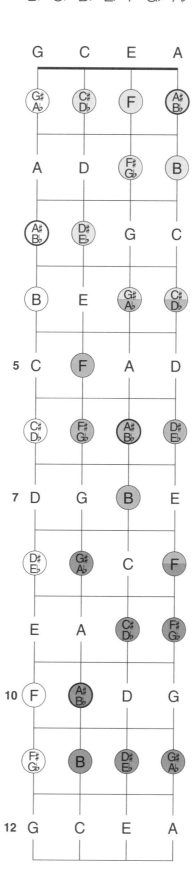

B PHRYGIAN

B–C–D–E–F♯–G–A

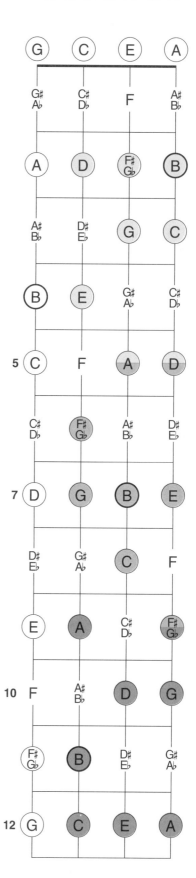

C LYDIAN

C–D–E–F#–G–A–B

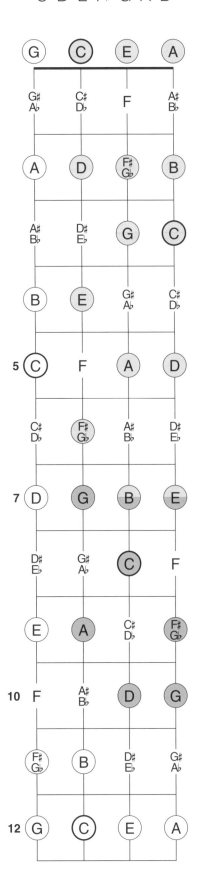

Db LYDIAN

Db–Eb–F–G–Ab–Bb–C

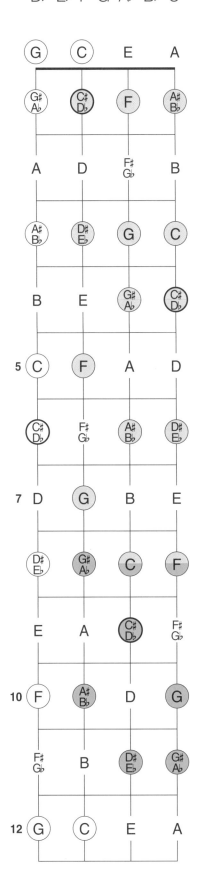

D LYDIAN

D–E–F#–G#–A–B–C#

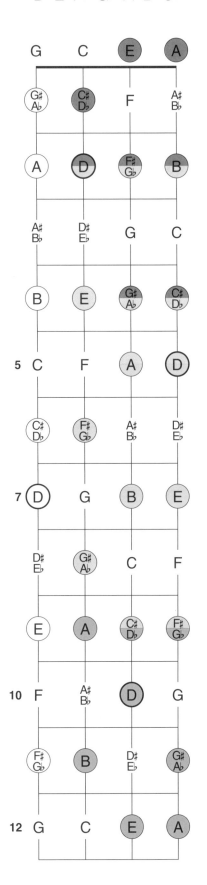

Eb LYDIAN

Eb–F–G–A–Bb–C–D

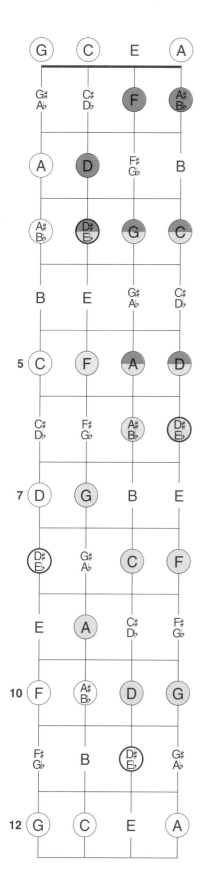

E LYDIAN

E–F#–G#–A#–B–C#–D#

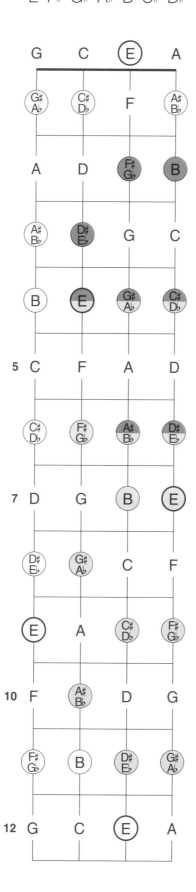

F LYDIAN

F–G–A–B–C–D–E

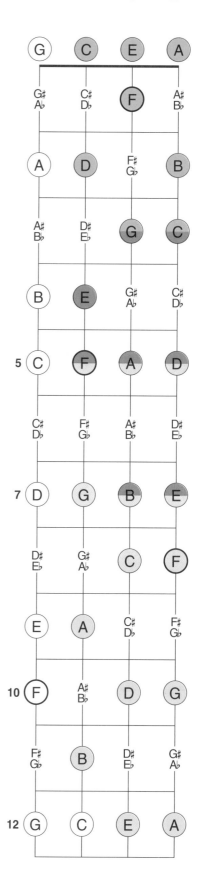

F♯/G♭ LYDIAN

F♯–G♯–A♯–B♯–C♯–D♯–E♯
G♭–A♭–B♭–C–D♭–E♭–F

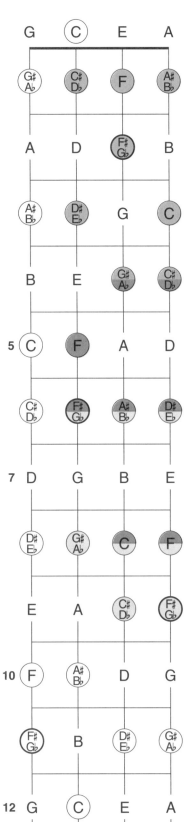

G LYDIAN

G–A–B–C♯–D–E–F♯

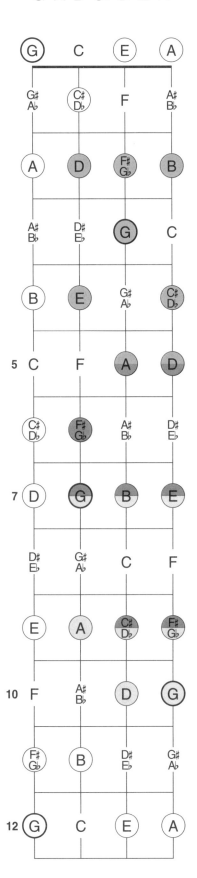

A♭ LYDIAN

A♭–B♭–C–D–E♭–F–G

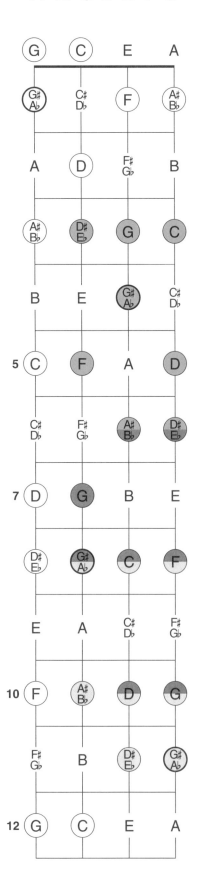

A LYDIAN

A–B–C#–D#–E–F#–G#

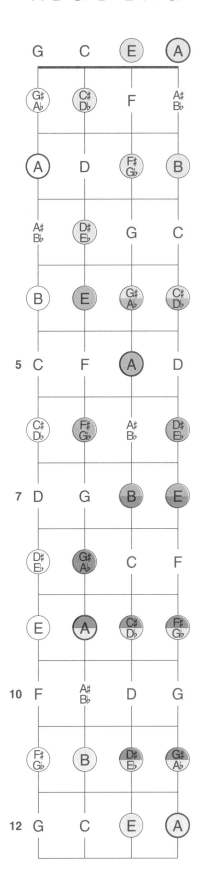

B♭ LYDIAN

B♭–C–D–E–F–G–A

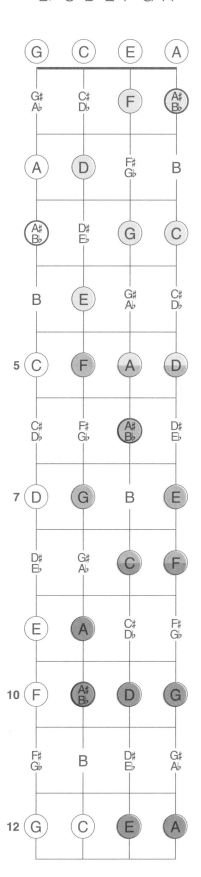

B LYDIAN

B–C#–D#–E#–F#–G#–A#

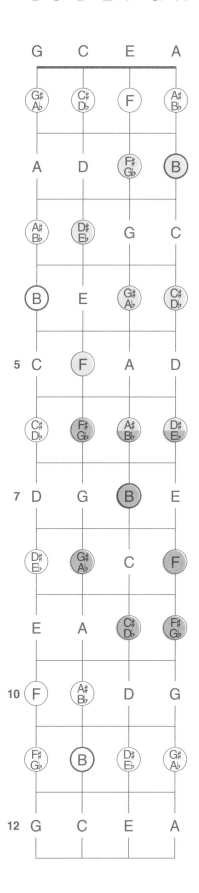

C MIXOLYDIAN

C–D–E–F–G–A–B♭

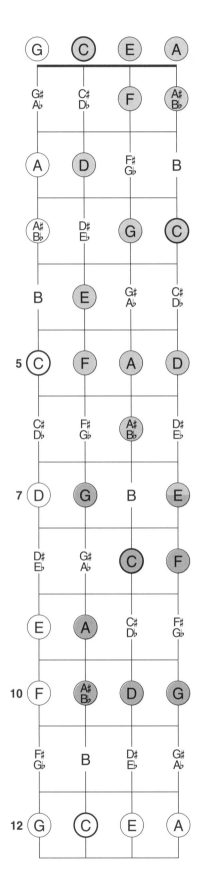

C♯/D♭ MIXOLYDIAN

C♯–D♯–E♯–F♯–G♯–A♯–B
D♭–E♭–F–G♭–A♭–B♭–C♭

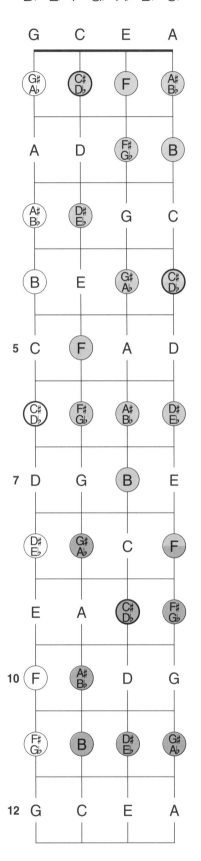

D MIXOLYDIAN

D–E–F♯–G–A–B–C

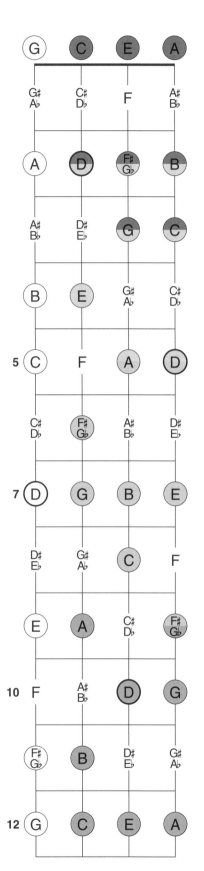

E♭ MIXOLYDIAN

E♭–F–G–A♭–B♭–C–D♭

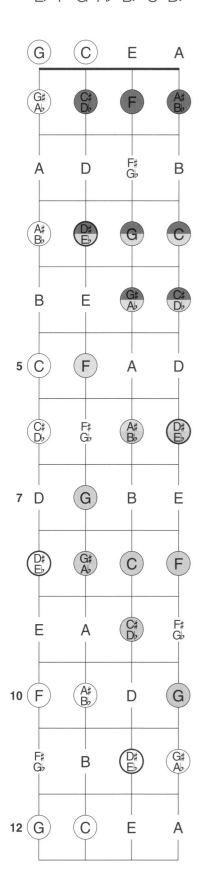

E MIXOLYDIAN

E–F♯–G♯–A–B–C♯–D

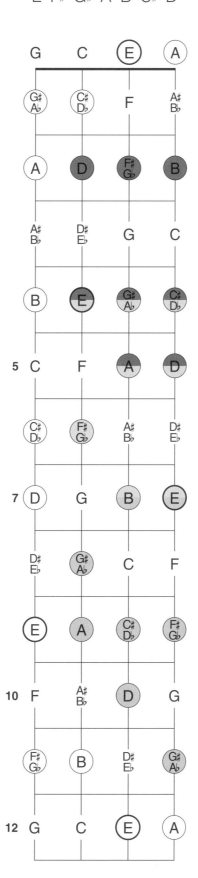

F MIXOLYDIAN

F–G–A–B♭–C–D–E♭

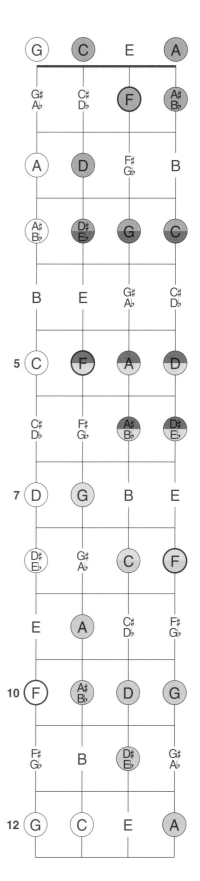

F#/Gb MIXOLYDIAN

F#–G#–A#–B–C#–D#–E
Gb–Ab–Bb–Cb–Db–Eb–Fb

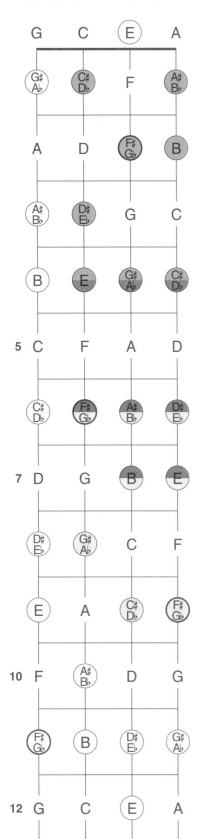

G MIXOLYDIAN

G–A–B–C–D–E–F

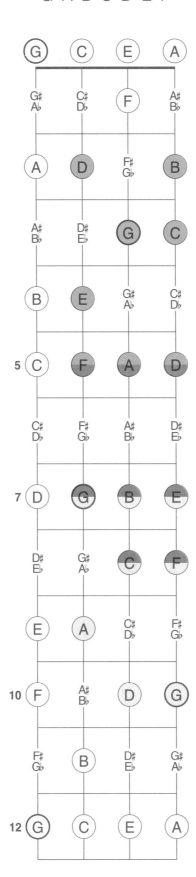

Ab MIXOLYDIAN

Ab–Bb–C–Db–Eb–F–Gb

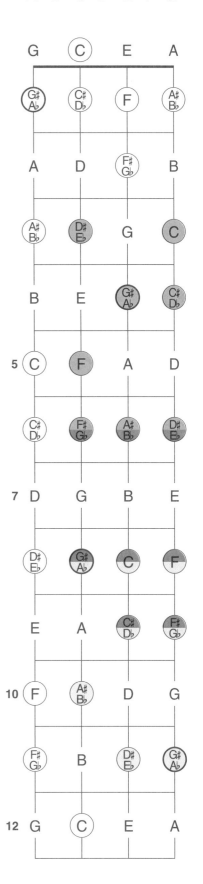

A MIXOLYDIAN

A–B–C#–D–E–F#–G

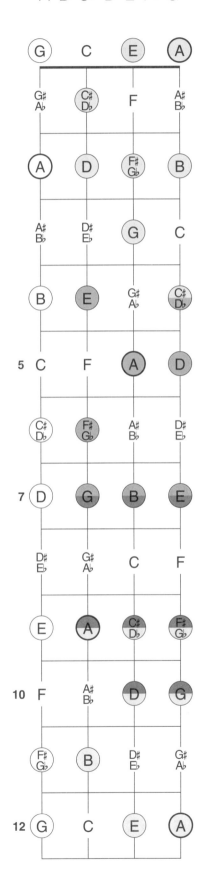

B♭ MIXOLYDIAN

B♭–C–D–E♭–F–G–A♭

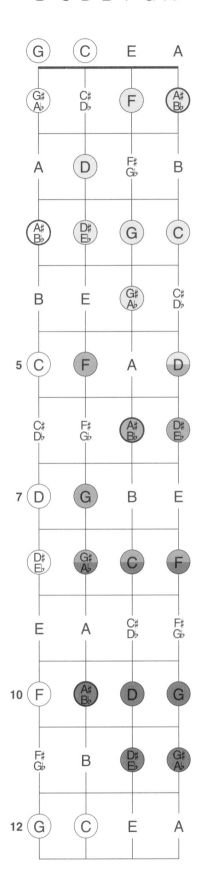

B MIXOLYDIAN

B–C#–D#–E–F#–G#–A

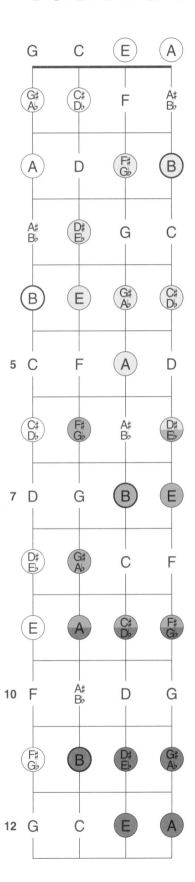

C AEOLIAN

C–D–E♭–F–G–A♭–B♭

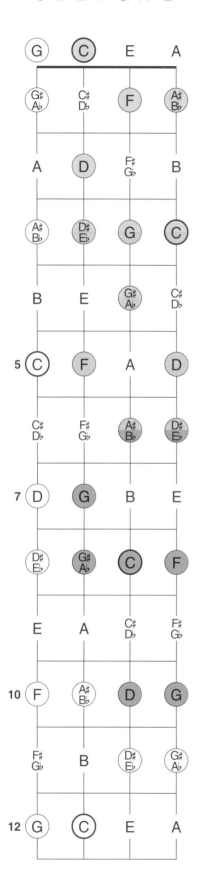

C♯ AEOLIAN

C♯–D♯–E–F♯–G♯–A–B

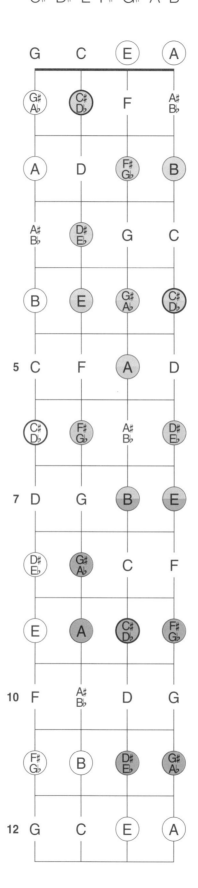

D AEOLIAN

D–E–F–G–A–B♭–C

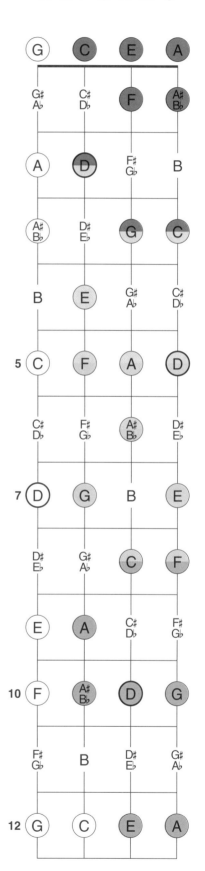

D#/E♭ AEOLIAN

D#–E#–F#–G#–A#–B–C#
E♭–F–G♭–A♭–B♭–C♭–D♭

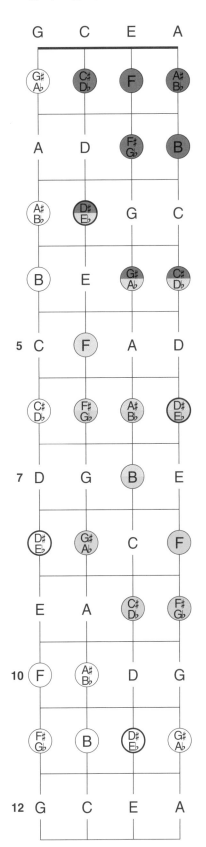

E AEOLIAN

E–F#–G–A–B–C–D

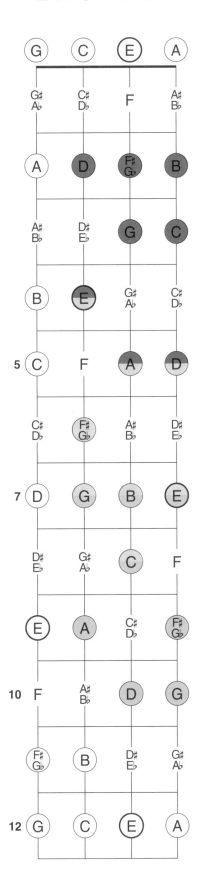

F AEOLIAN

F–G–A♭–B♭–C–D♭–E♭

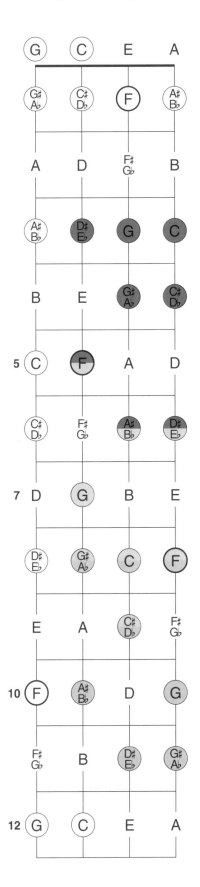

F♯ AEOLIAN

F♯–G♯–A–B–C♯–D–E

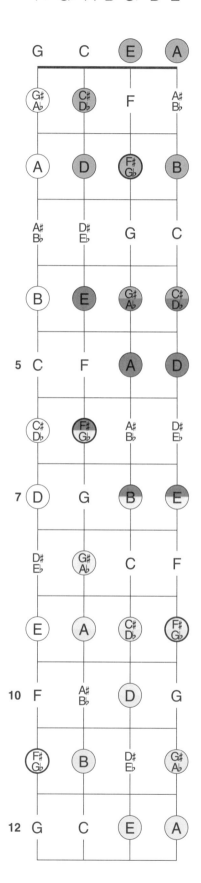

G AEOLIAN

G–A–B♭–C–D–E♭–F

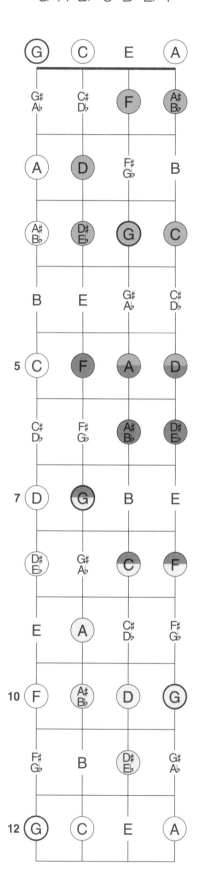

A♭ AEOLIAN

A♭–B♭–C♭–D♭–E♭–F♭–G♭

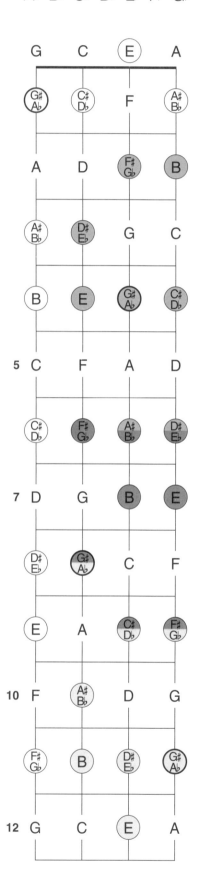

A AEOLIAN

A–B–C–D–E–F–G

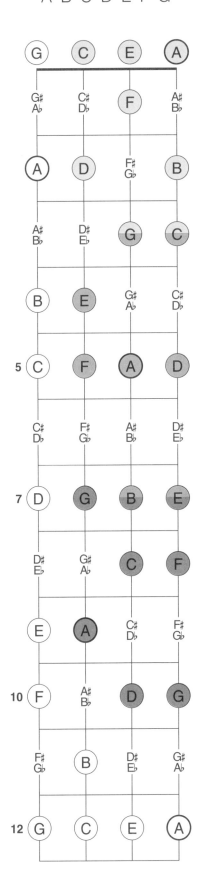

B♭ AEOLIAN

B♭–C–D♭–E♭–F–G♭–A♭

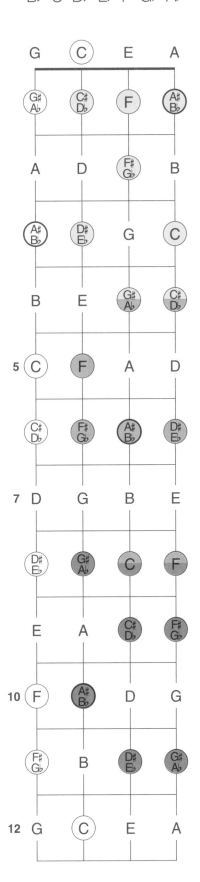

B AEOLIAN

B–C#–D–E–F#–G–A

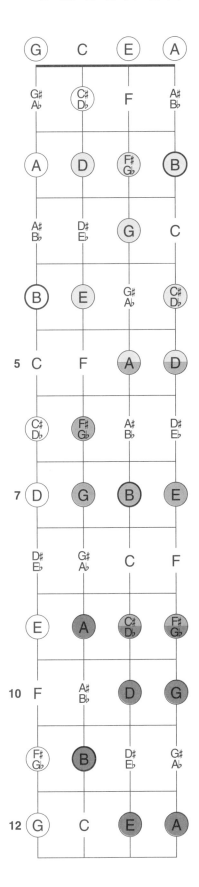

31

C LOCRIAN

C–Db–Eb–F–Gb–Ab–Bb

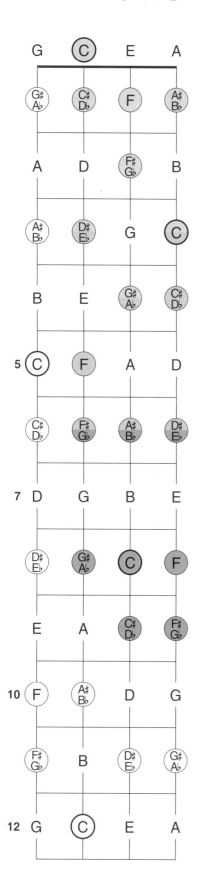

C# LOCRIAN

C#–D–E–F#–G–A–B

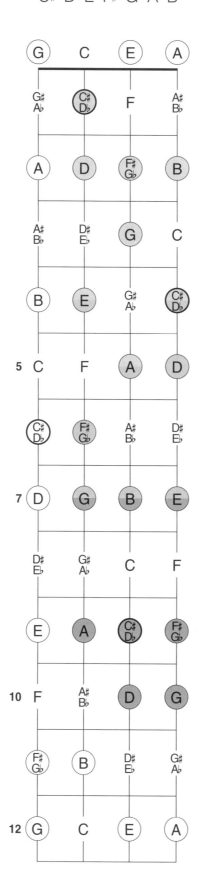

D LOCRIAN

D–Eb–F–G–Ab–Bb–C

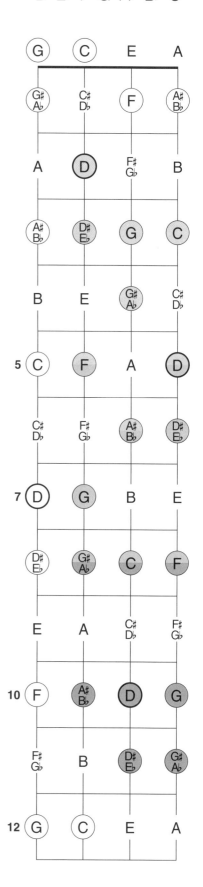

D♯ LOCRIAN

D♯–E–F♯–G♯–A–B–C♯

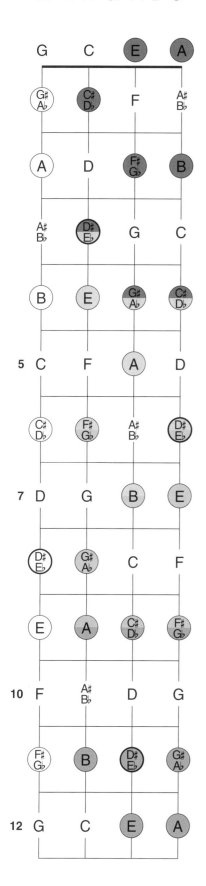

E LOCRIAN

E–F–G–A–B♭–C–D

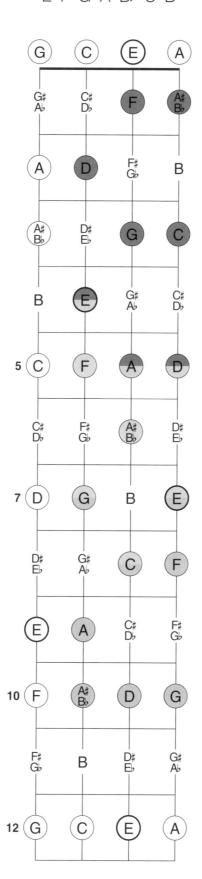

F LOCRIAN

F–G♭–A♭–B♭–C♭–D♭–E♭

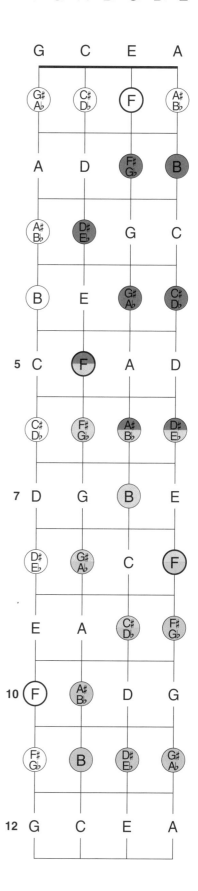

F# LOCRIAN

F#–G–A–B–C–D–E

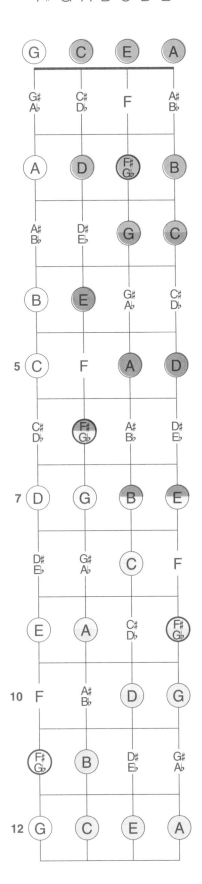

G LOCRIAN

G–Ab–Bb–C–Db–Eb–F

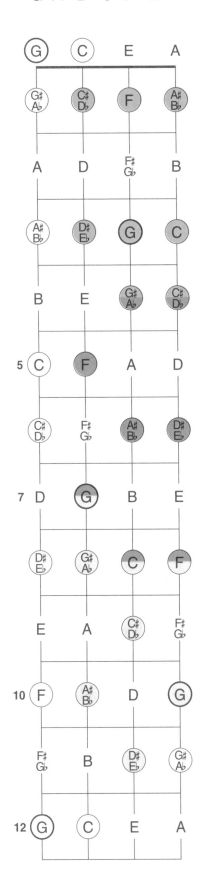

G# LOCRIAN

G#–A–B–C#–D–E–F#

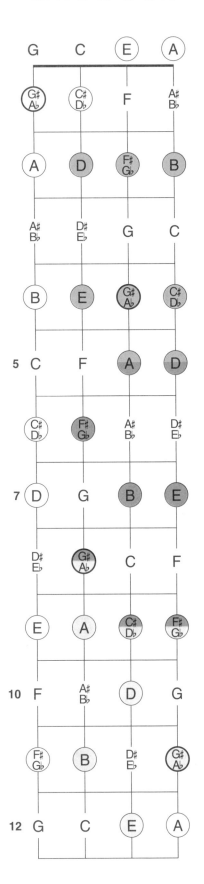

A LOCRIAN

A–B♭–C–D–E♭–F–G

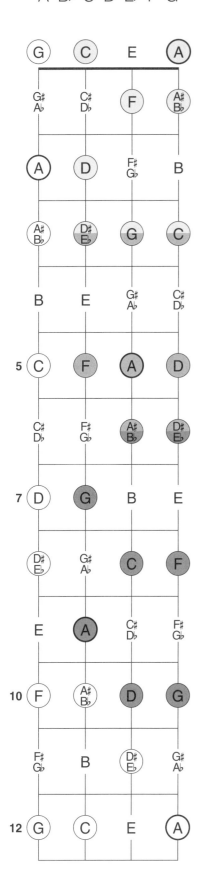

A♯ LOCRIAN

A♯–B–C♯–D♯–E–F♯–G♯

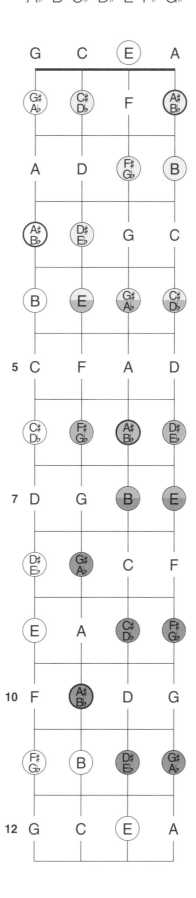

B LOCRIAN

B–C–D–E–F–G–A

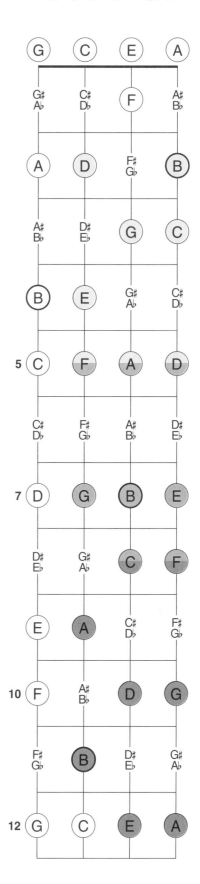

SCALES

PENTATONIC AND BLUES SCALES

C MAJOR PENTATONIC

C–D–E–G–A

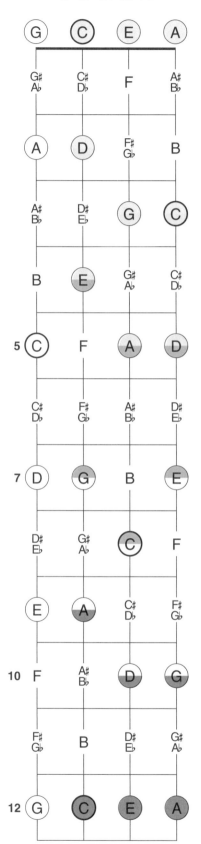

D♭ MAJOR PENTATONIC

D♭–E♭–F–A♭–B♭

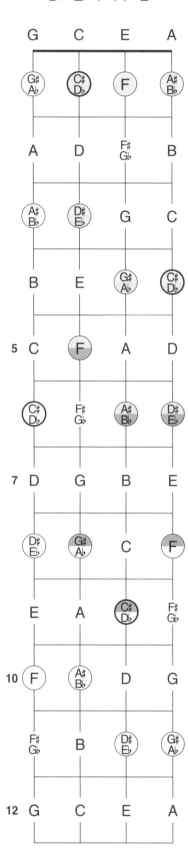

D MAJOR PENTATONIC

D–E–F#–A–B

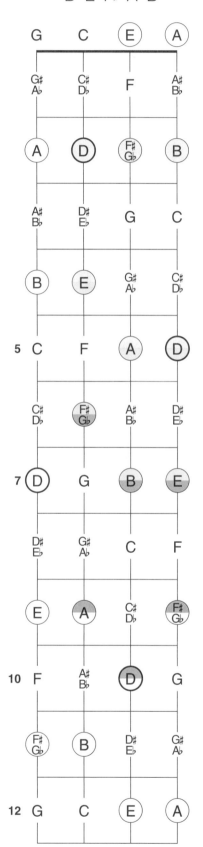

Eb MAJOR PENTATONIC

Eb–F–G–Bb–C

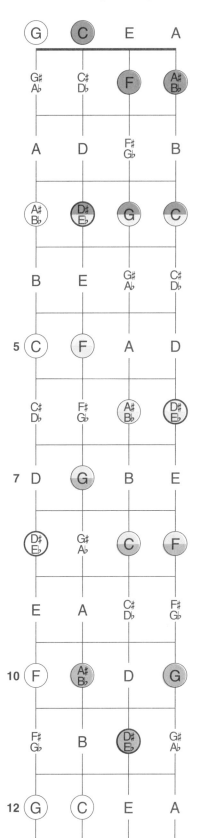

E MAJOR PENTATONIC

E–F#–G#–B–C#

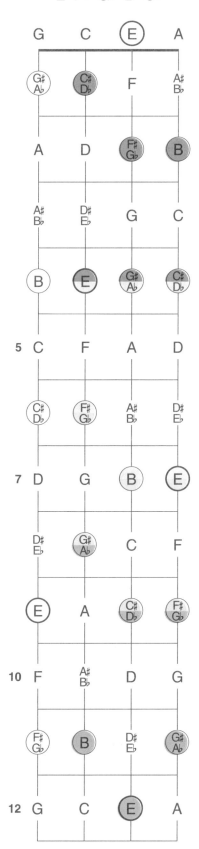

F MAJOR PENTATONIC

F–G–A–C–D

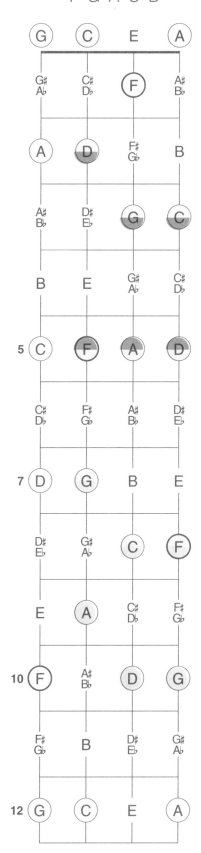

G♭ MAJOR PENTATONIC

G♭–A♭–B♭–D♭–E♭

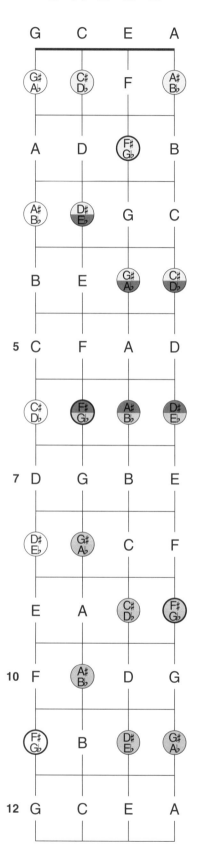

G MAJOR PENTATONIC

G–A–B–D–E

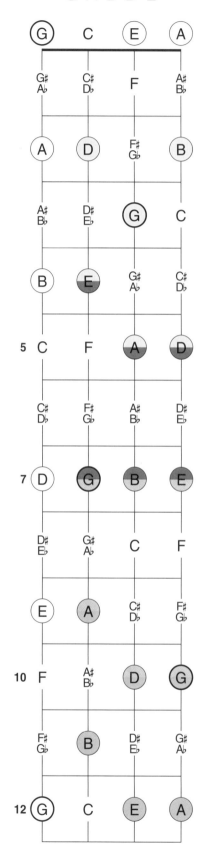

A♭ MAJOR PENTATONIC

A♭–B♭–C–E♭–F

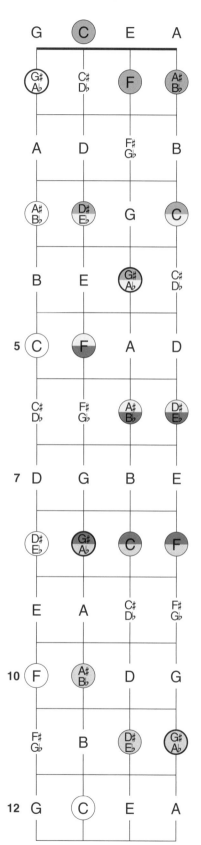

A MAJOR PENTATONIC

A–B–C#–E–F#

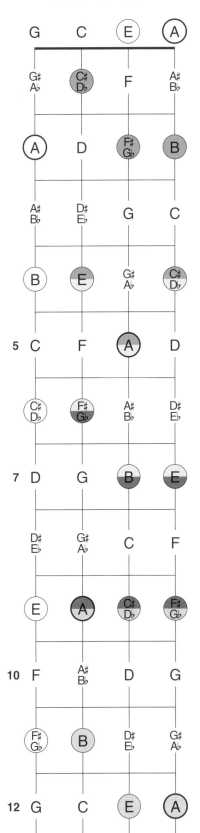

Bb MAJOR PENTATONIC

Bb–C–D–F–G

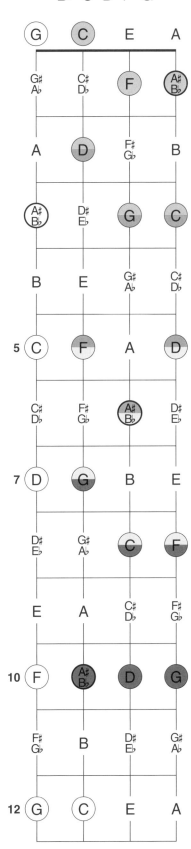

B MAJOR PENTATONIC

B–C#–D#–F#–G#

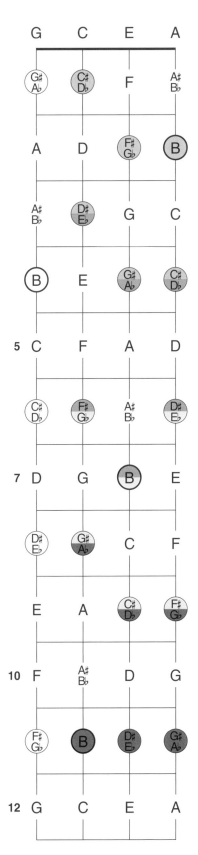

C MINOR PENTATONIC

C–E♭–F–G–B♭

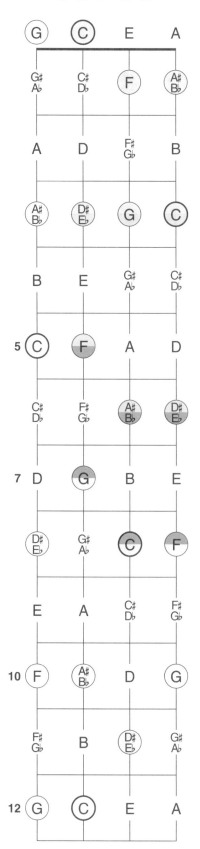

C♯ MINOR PENTATONIC

C♯–E–F♯–G♯–B

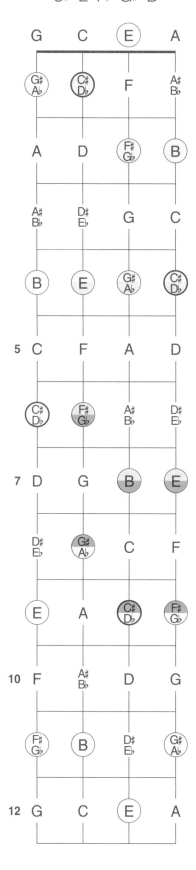

D MINOR PENTATONIC

D–F–G–A–C

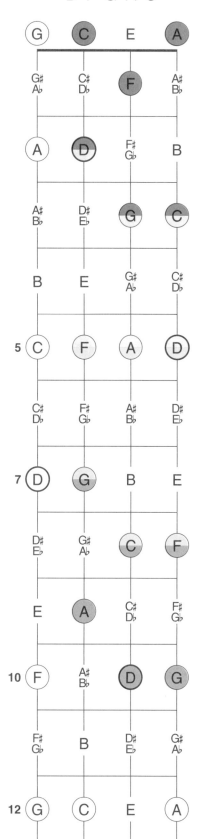

Eb MINOR PENTATONIC

Eb–Gb–Ab–Bb–Db

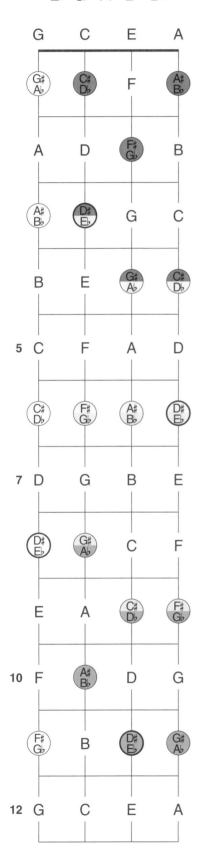

E MINOR PENTATONIC

E–G–A–B–D

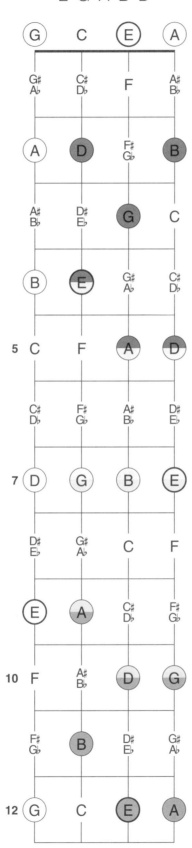

F MINOR PENTATONIC

F–Ab–Bb–C–Eb

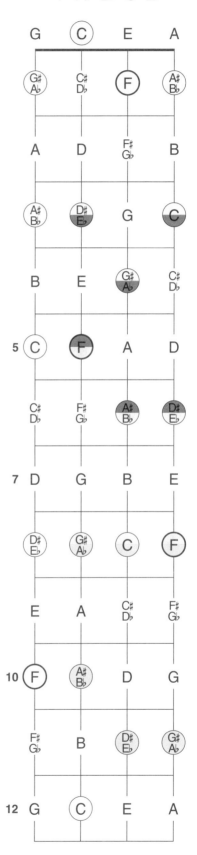

F# MINOR PENTATONIC

F#–A–B–C#–E

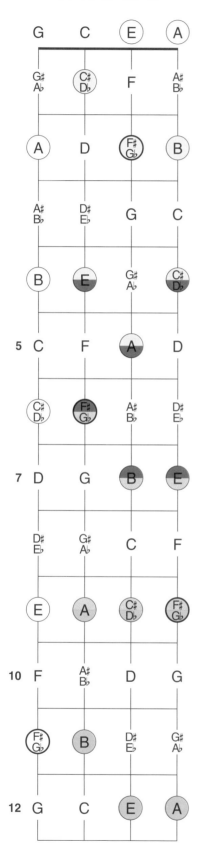

G MINOR PENTATONIC

G–B♭–C–D–F

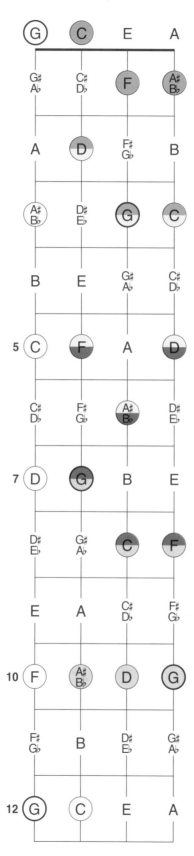

A♭ MINOR PENTATONIC

A♭–C♭–D♭–E♭–G♭

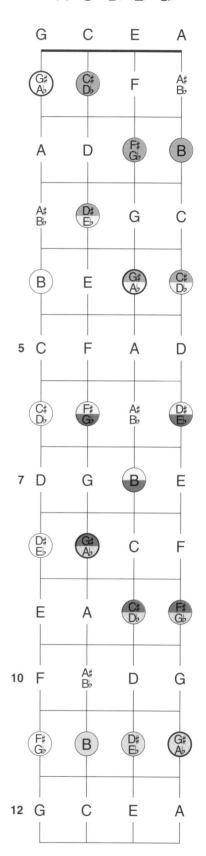

A MINOR PENTATONIC

A–C–D–E–G

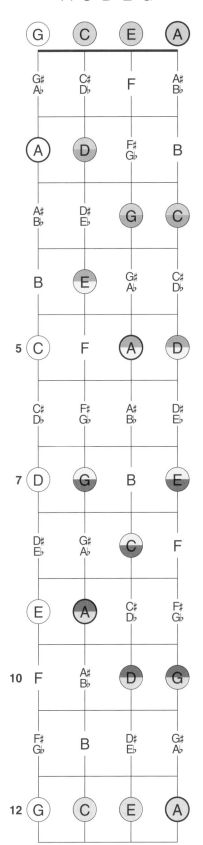

B♭ MINOR PENTATONIC

B♭–D♭–E♭–F–A♭

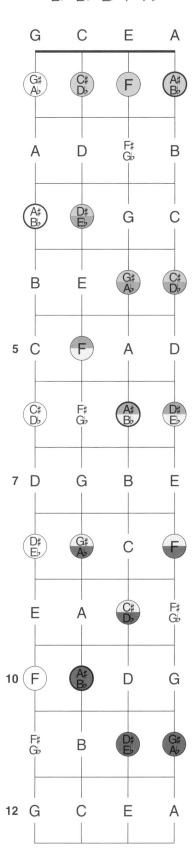

B MINOR PENTATONIC

B–D–E–F♯–A

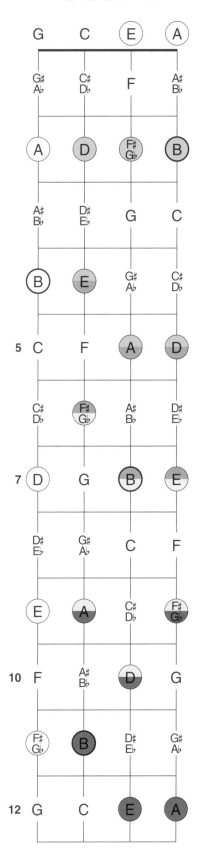

C BLUES

C–E♭–F–G♭–G–B♭

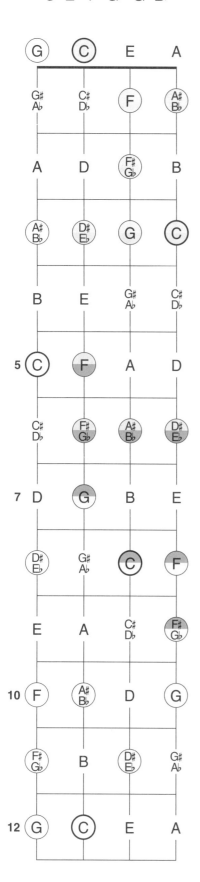

C♯ BLUES

C♯–E–F♯–G–G♯–B

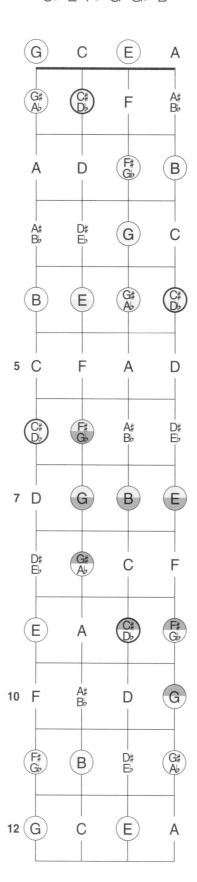

D BLUES

D–F–G–A♭–A–C

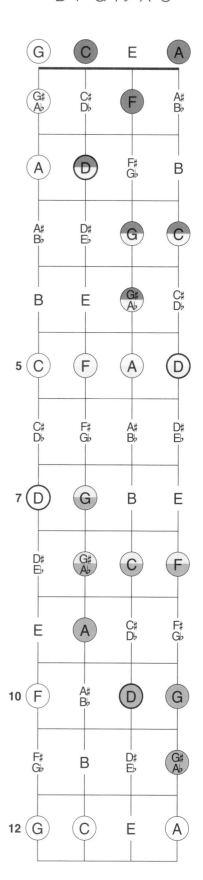

Eb BLUES

Eb–Gb–Ab–A–Bb–Db

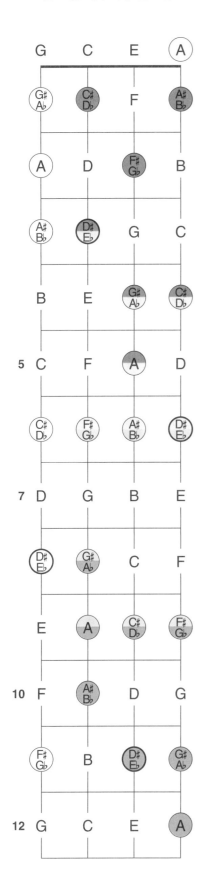

E BLUES

E–G–A–Bb–B–D

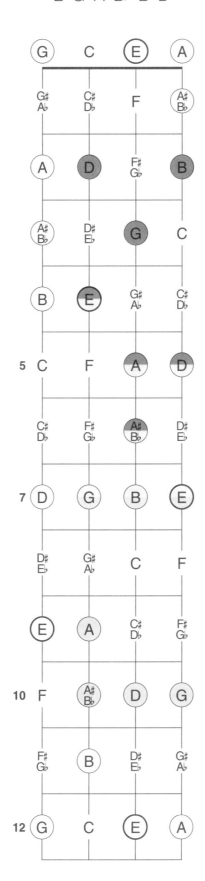

F BLUES

F–Ab–Bb–Cb–C–Eb

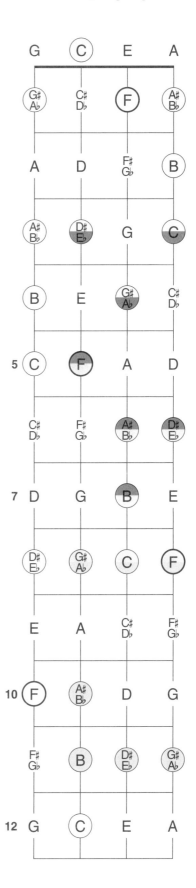

F# BLUES

F#–A–B–C–C#–E

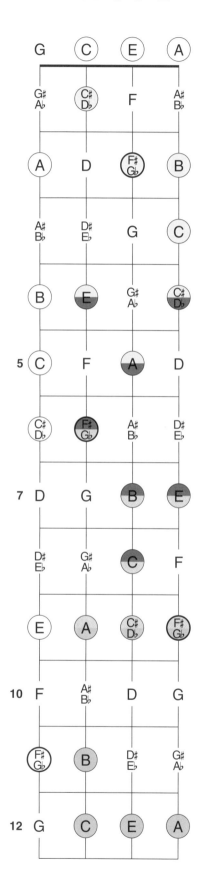

G BLUES

G–Bb–C–Db–D–F

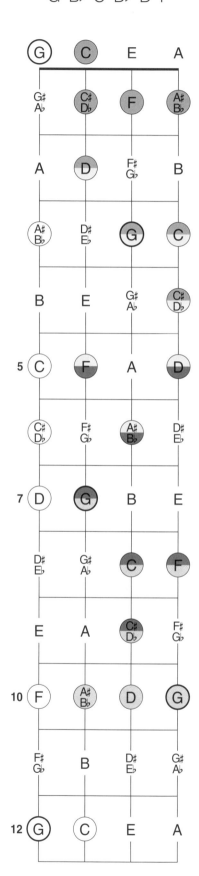

Ab BLUES

Ab–Cb–Db–D–Eb–Gb

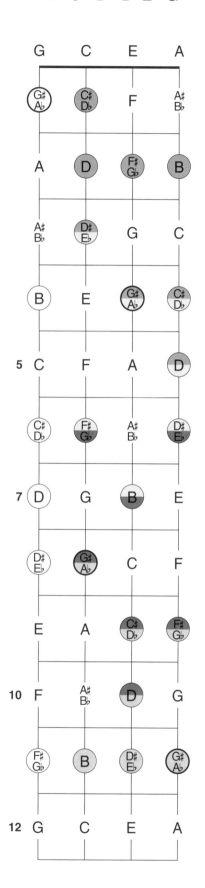

A BLUES

A–C–D–E♭–E–G

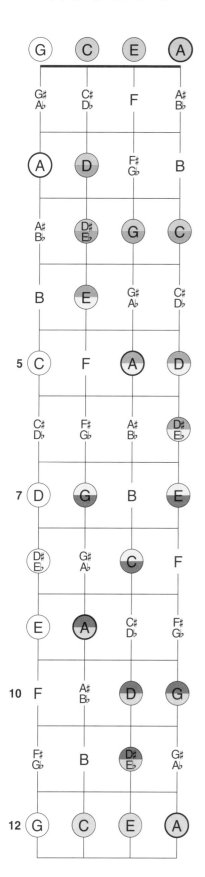

B♭ BLUES

B♭–D♭–E♭–E–F–A♭

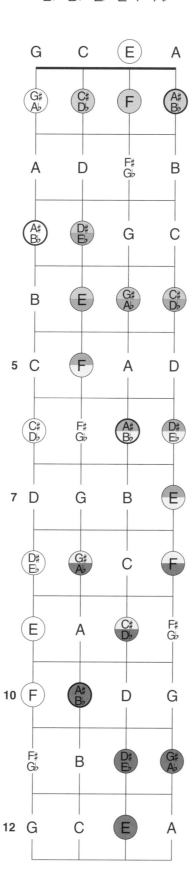

B BLUES

B–D–E–F–F♯–A

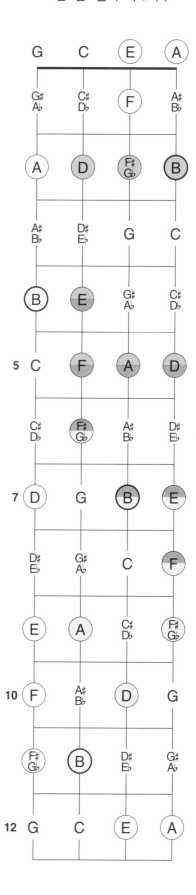

SCALES

THE MELODIC MINOR SCALE AND SELECT MODES

C MELODIC MINOR

C–D–E♭–F–G–A–B

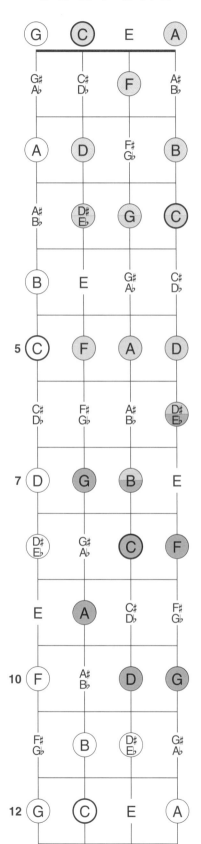

C♯ MELODIC MINOR

C♯–D♯–E–F♯–G♯–A♯–B♯

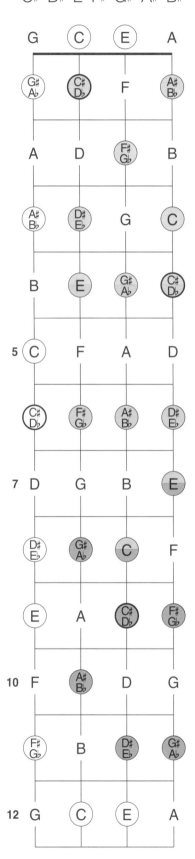

D MELODIC MINOR

D–E–F–G–A–B–C♯

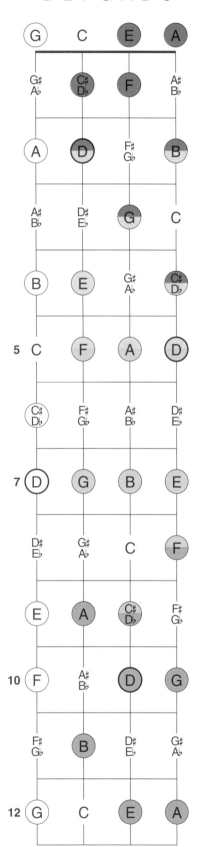

E♭ MELODIC MINOR

E♭–F–G♭–A♭–B♭–C–D

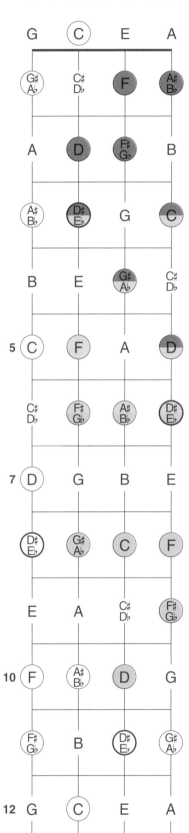

E MELODIC MINOR

E–F♯–G–A–B–C♯–D♯

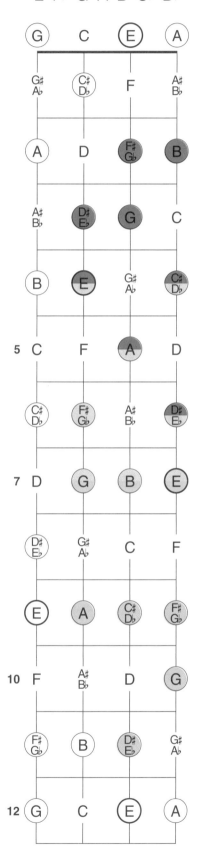

F MELODIC MINOR

F–G–A♭–B♭–C–D–E

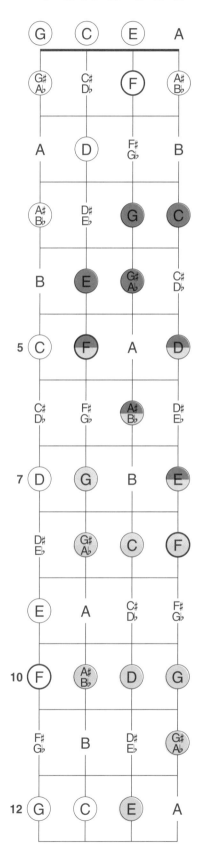

F# MELODIC MINOR

F#–G#–A–B–C#–D#–E#

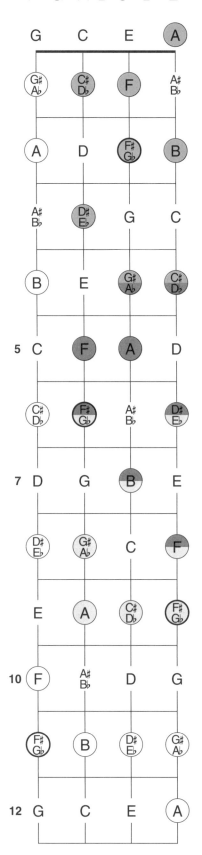

G MELODIC MINOR

G–A–B♭–C–D–E–F#

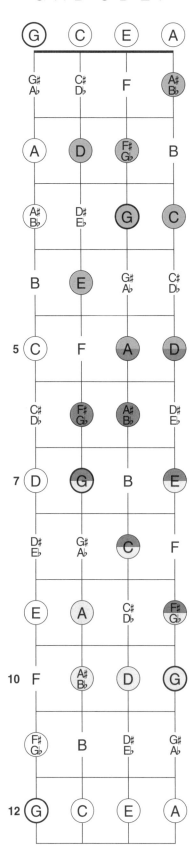

A♭ MELODIC MINOR

A♭–B♭–C♭–D♭–E♭–F–G

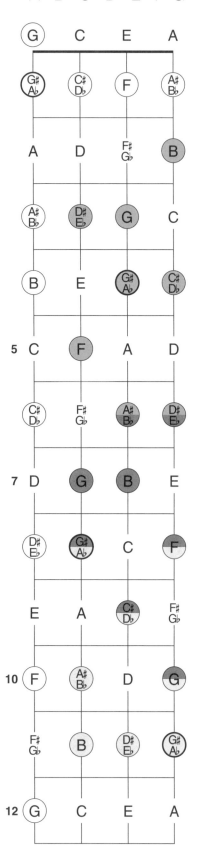

A MELODIC MINOR

A–B–C–D–E–F#–G#

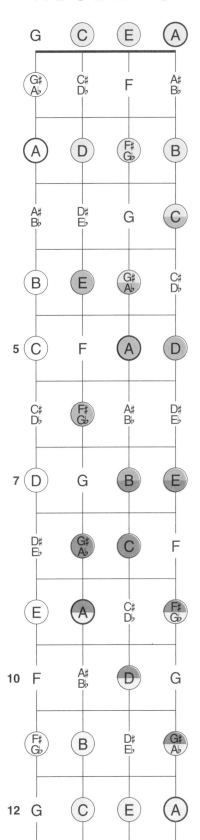

B♭ MELODIC MINOR

B♭–C–D♭–E♭–F–G–A

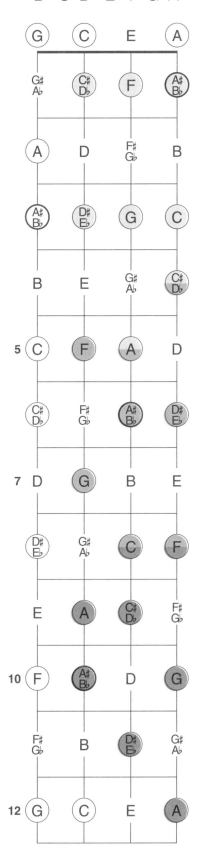

B MELODIC MINOR

B–C#–D–E–F#–G#–A#

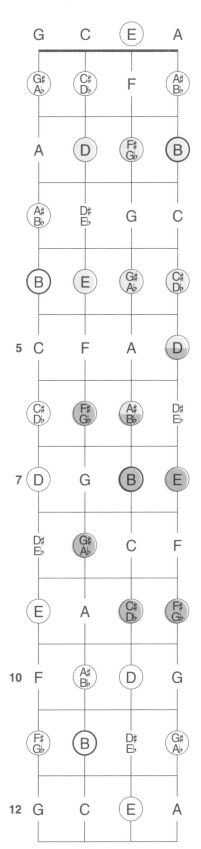

C LYDIAN DOMINANT

C–D–E–F♯–G–A–B♭

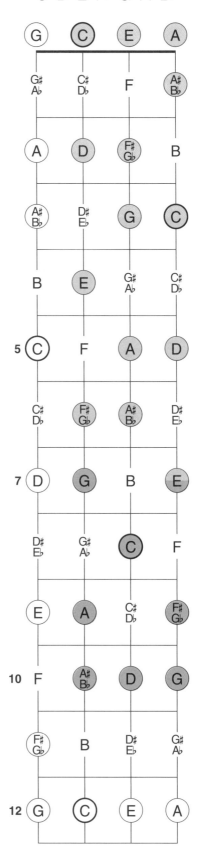

D♭ LYDIAN DOMINANT

D♭–E♭–F–G–A♭–B♭–C♭

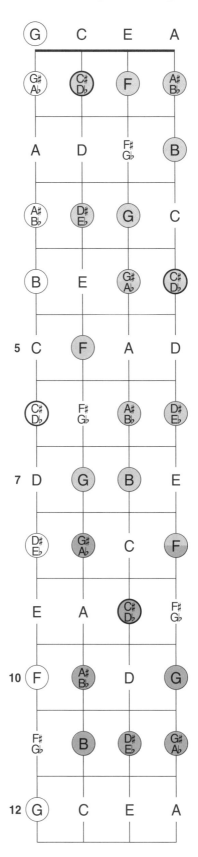

D LYDIAN DOMINANT

D–E–F♯–G♯–A–B–C

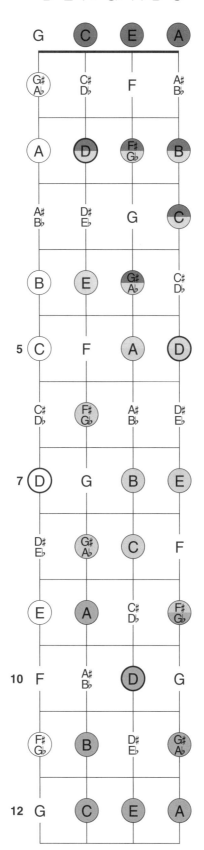

E♭ LYDIAN DOMINANT

E♭–F–G–A–B♭–C–D♭

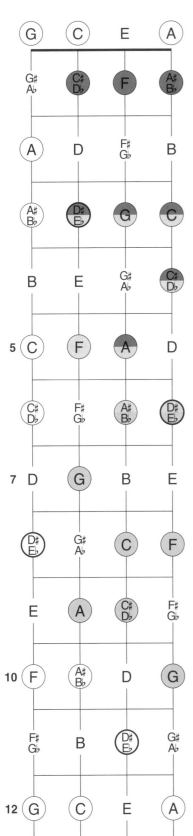

E LYDIAN DOMINANT

E–F#–G#–A#–B–C#–D

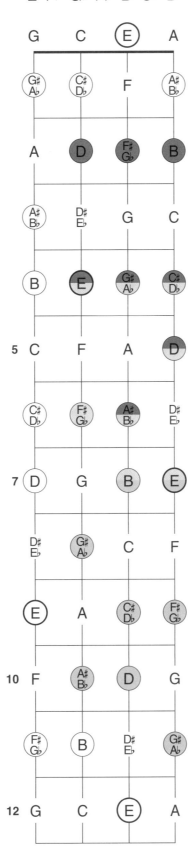

F LYDIAN DOMINANT

F–G–A–B–C–D–E♭

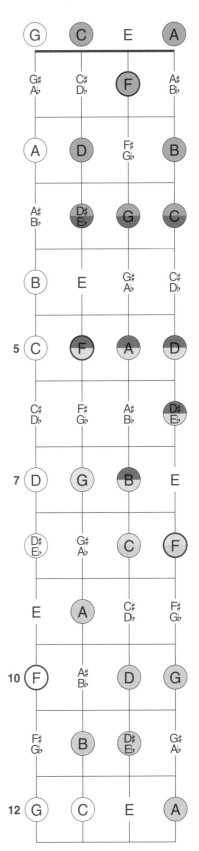

G♭ LYDIAN DOMINANT

G♭–A♭–B♭–C–D♭–E♭–F♭

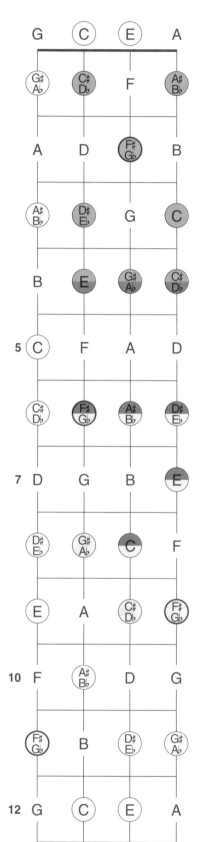

G LYDIAN DOMINANT

G–A–B–C♯–D–E–F

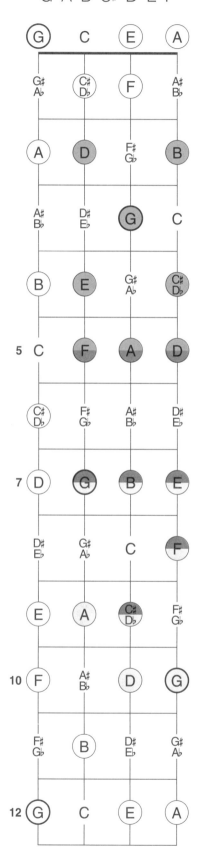

A♭ LYDIAN DOMINANT

A♭–B♭–C–D–E♭–F–G♭

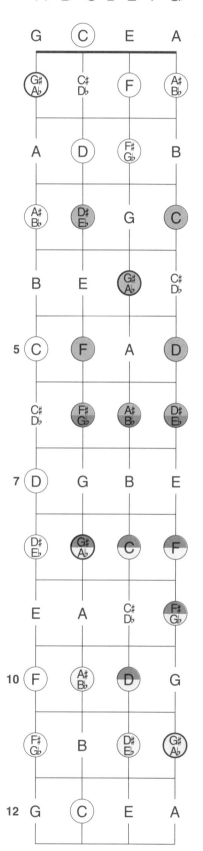

A LYDIAN DOMINANT

A–B–C#–D#–E–F#–G

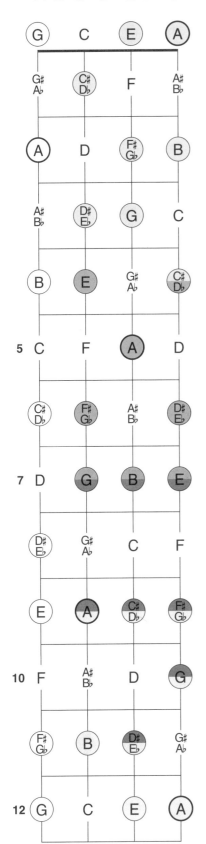

B♭ LYDIAN DOMINANT

B♭–C–D–E–F–G–A♭

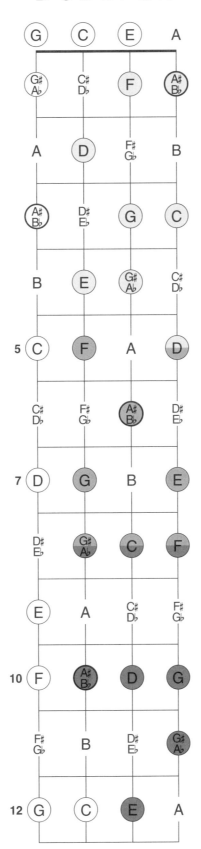

B LYDIAN DOMINANT

B–C#–D#–E#–F#–G#–A

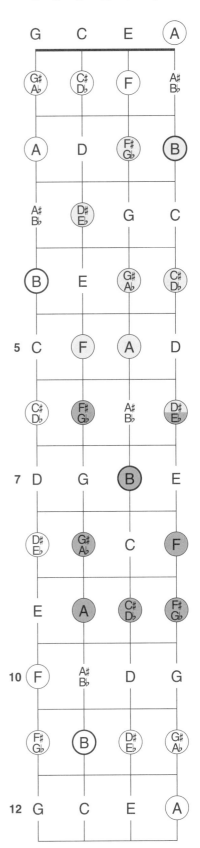

C SUPER LOCRIAN

C–Db–Eb–Fb–Gb–Ab–Bb

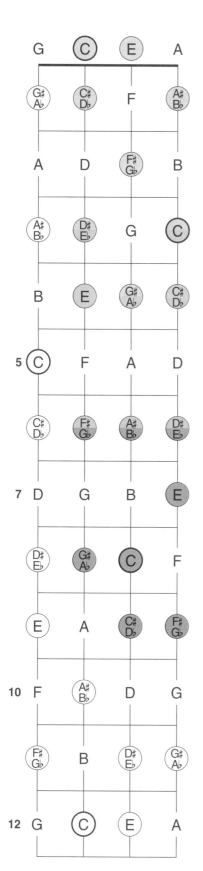

C# SUPER LOCRIAN

C#–D–E–F–G–A–B

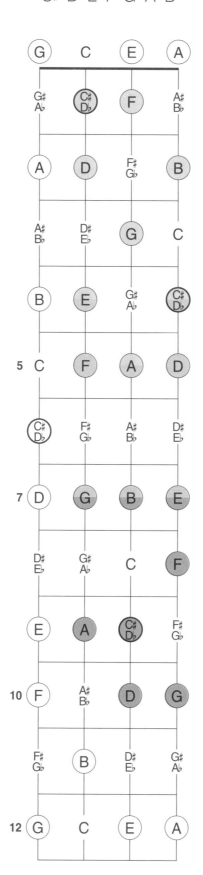

D SUPER LOCRIAN

D–Eb–F–Gb–Ab–Bb–C

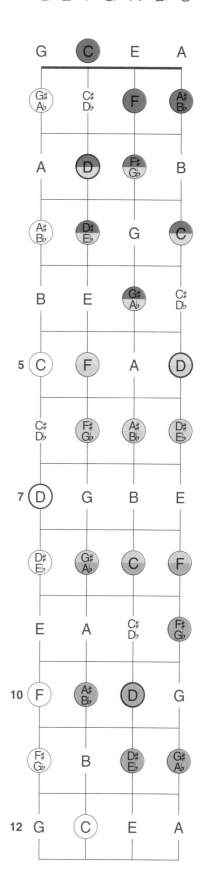

D# SUPER LOCRIAN

D#–E–F#–G–A–B–C#

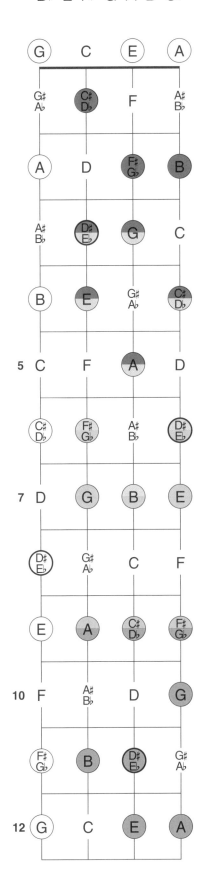

E SUPER LOCRIAN

E–F–G–A♭–B♭–C–D

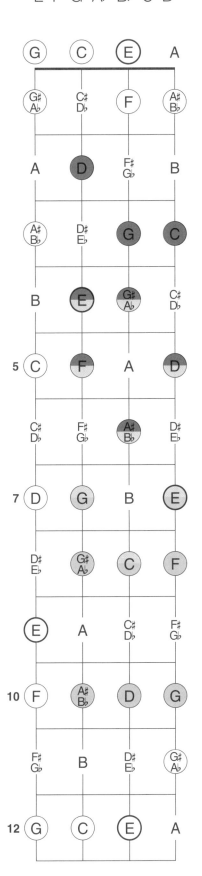

F SUPER LOCRIAN

F–G♭–A♭–B♭♭–C♭–D♭–E♭

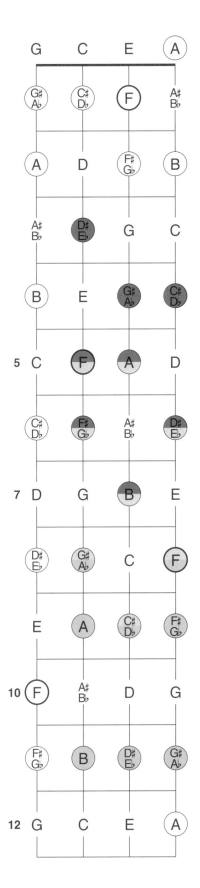

F♯ SUPER LOCRIAN

F♯–G–A–B♭–C–D–E

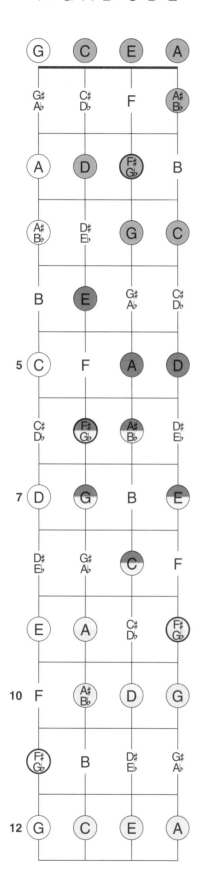

G SUPER LOCRIAN

G–A♭–B♭–C♭–D♭–E♭–F

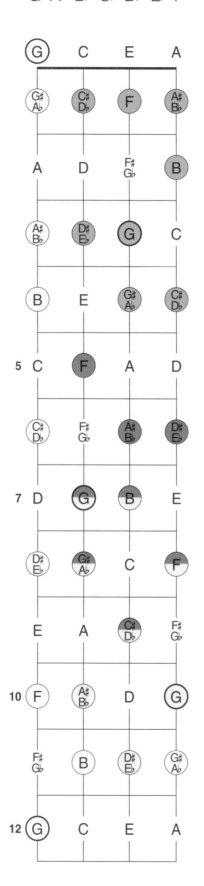

G♯ SUPER LOCRIAN

G♯–A–B–C–D–E–F♯

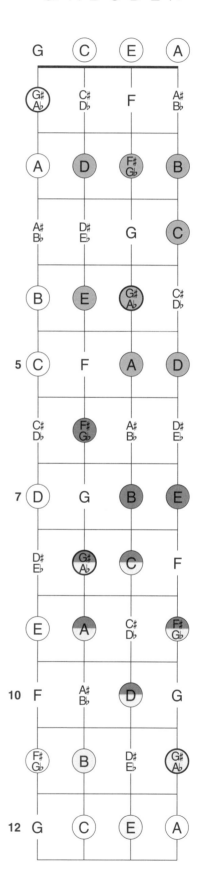

A SUPER LOCRIAN

A–B♭–C–D♭–E♭–F–G

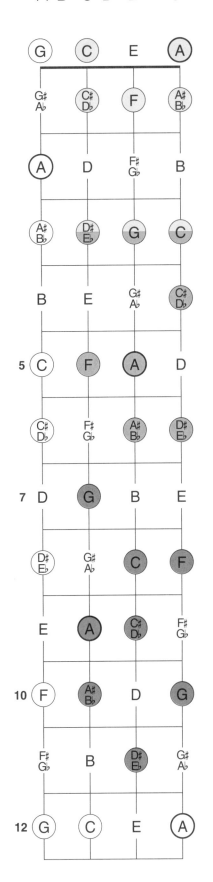

A♯ SUPER LOCRIAN

A♯–B–C♯–D–E–F♯–G♯

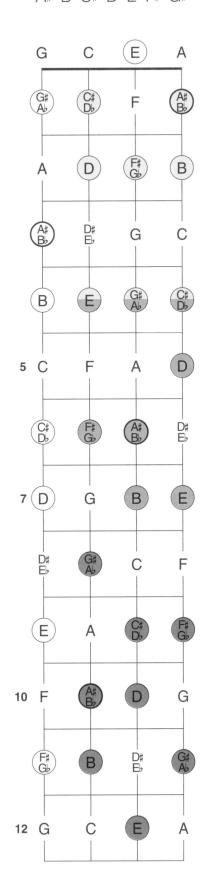

B SUPER LOCRIAN

B–C–D–E♭–F–G–A

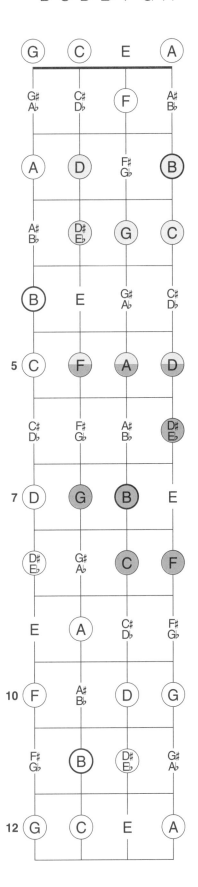

SCALES

THE HARMONIC MINOR SCALE AND SELECT MODE

C HARMONIC MINOR

C–D–E♭–F–G–A♭–B

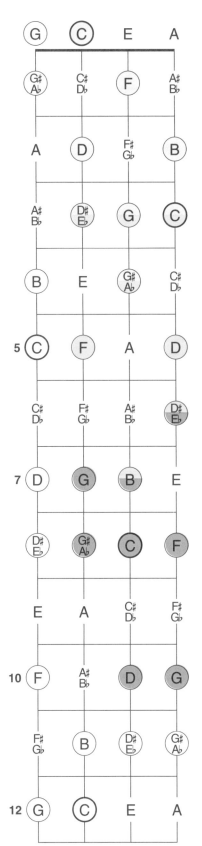

C♯ HARMONIC MINOR

C♯–D♯–E–F♯–G♯–A–B♯

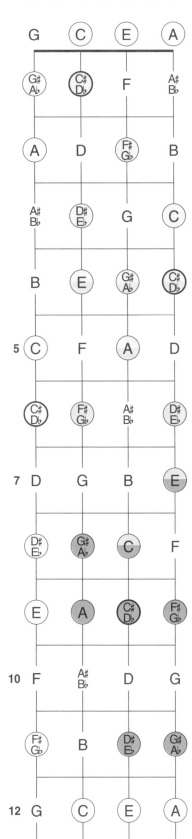

D HARMONIC MINOR

D–E–F–G–A–B♭–C♯

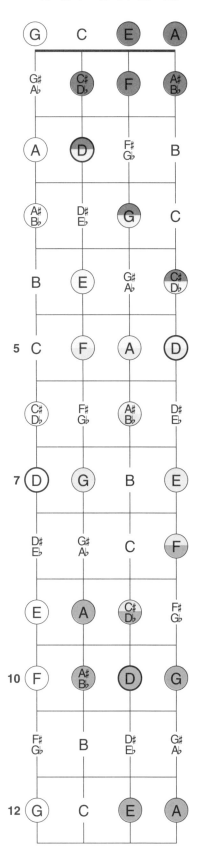

E♭ HARMONIC MINOR

E♭–F–G♭–A♭–B♭–C♭–D

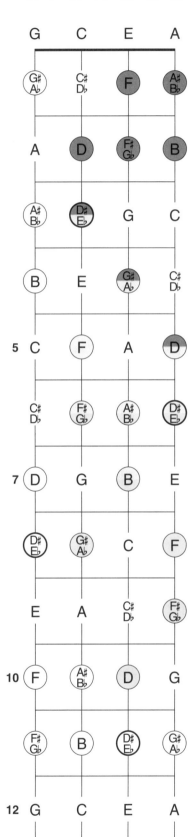

E HARMONIC MINOR

E–F#–G–A–B–C–D#

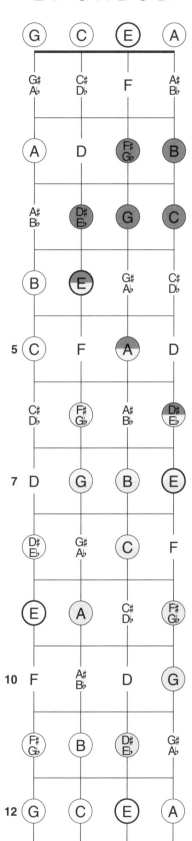

F HARMONIC MINOR

F–G–A♭–B♭–C–D♭–E

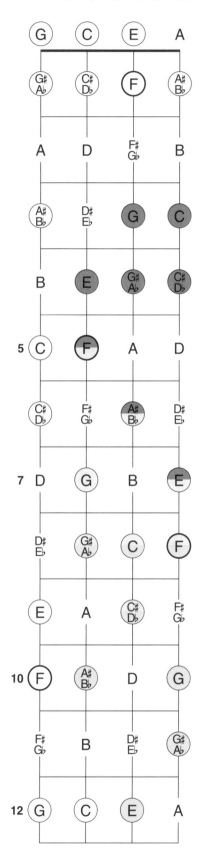

F# HARMONIC MINOR

F#–G#–A–B–C#–D–E#

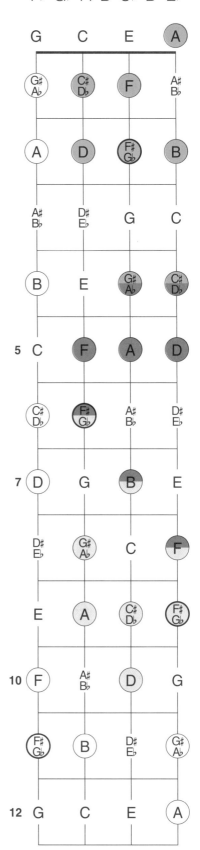

G HARMONIC MINOR

G–A–B♭–C–D–E♭–F#

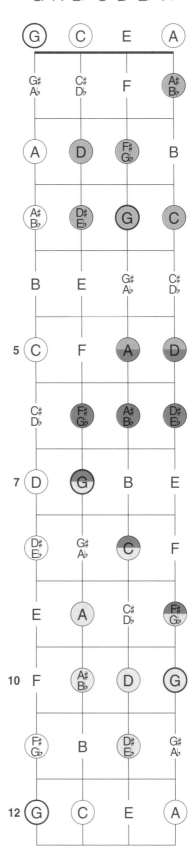

A♭ HARMONIC MINOR

A♭–B♭–C♭–D♭–E♭–F♭–G

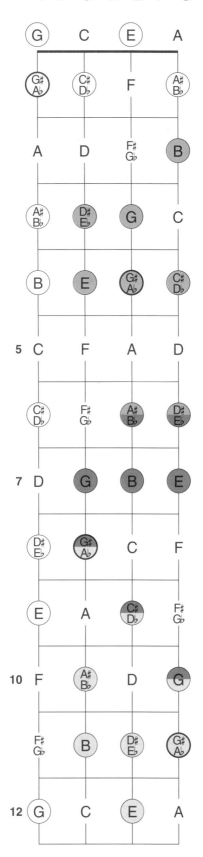

A HARMONIC MINOR

A–B–C–D–E–F–G#

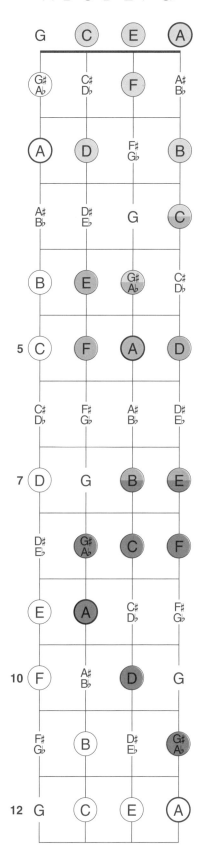

Bb HARMONIC MINOR

Bb–C–Db–Eb–F–Gb–A

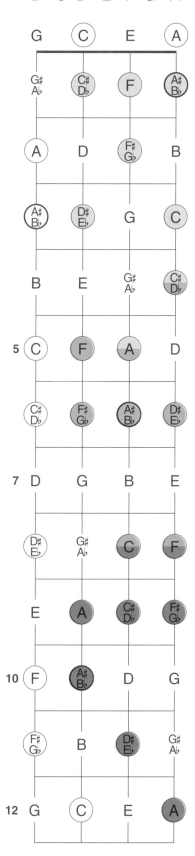

B HARMONIC MINOR

B–C#–D–E–F#–G–A#

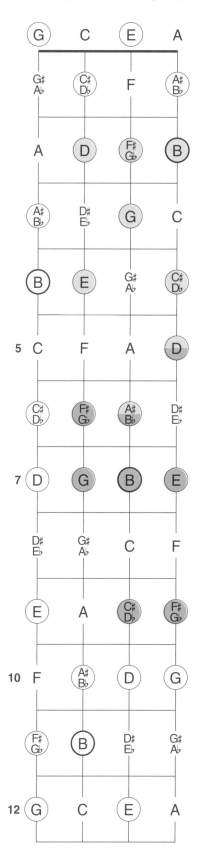

C PHRYGIAN DOMINANT

C–Db–E–F–G–Ab–Bb

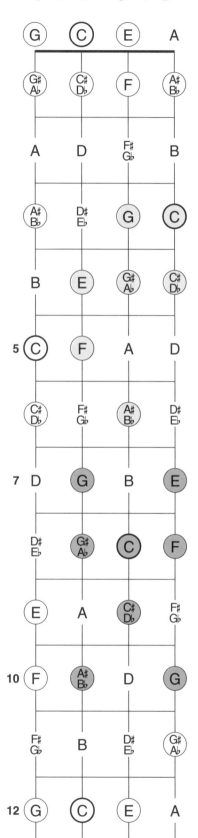

C♯ PHRYGIAN DOMINANT

C#–D–E#–F#–G#–A–B

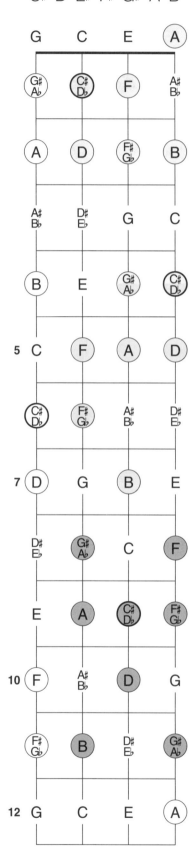

D PHRYGIAN DOMINANT

D–Eb–F#–G–A–Bb–C

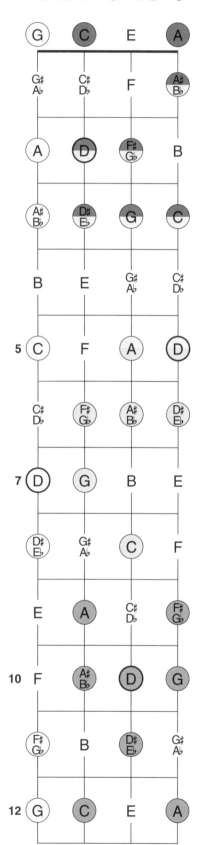

E♭ PHRYGIAN DOMINANT

E♭–F♭–G–A♭–B♭–C♭–D♭

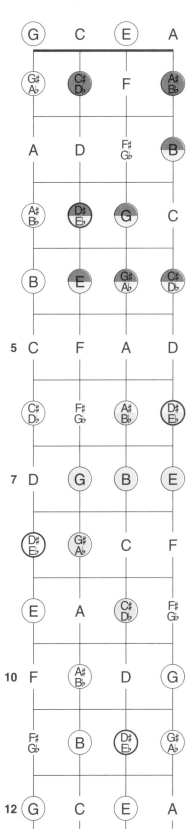

E PHRYGIAN DOMINANT

E–F–G#–A–B–C–D

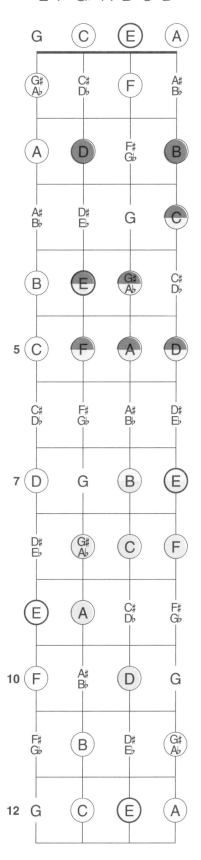

F PHRYGIAN DOMINANT

F–G♭–A–B♭–C–D♭–E♭

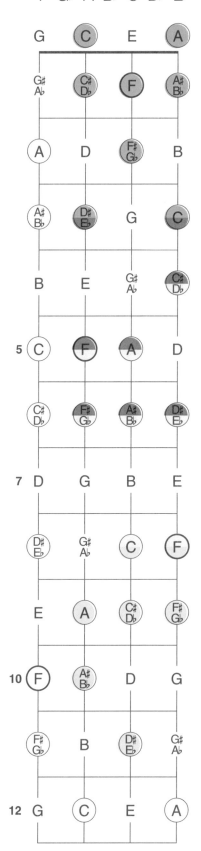

F# PHRYGIAN DOMINANT

F#–G–A#–B–C#–D–E

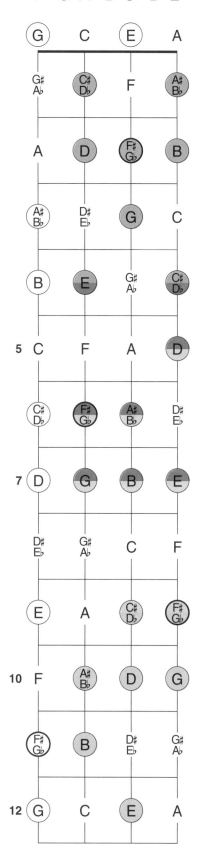

G PHRYGIAN DOMINANT

G–Ab–B–C–D–Eb–F

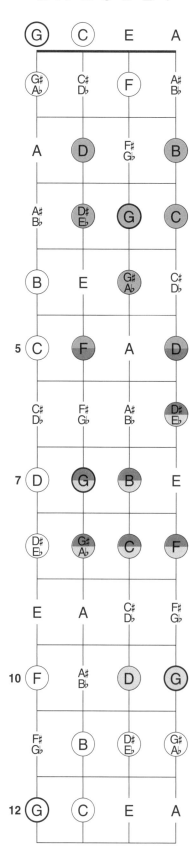

G# PHRYGIAN DOMINANT

G#–A–B#–C#–D#–E–F#

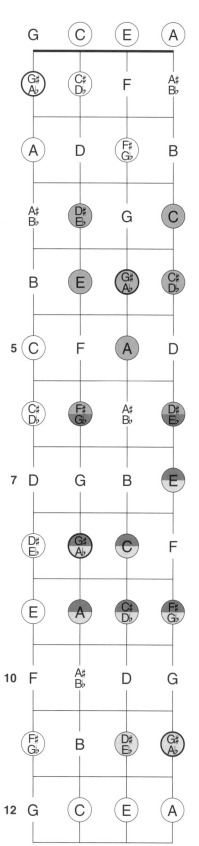

A PHRYGIAN DOMINANT

A–B♭–C♯–D–E–F–G

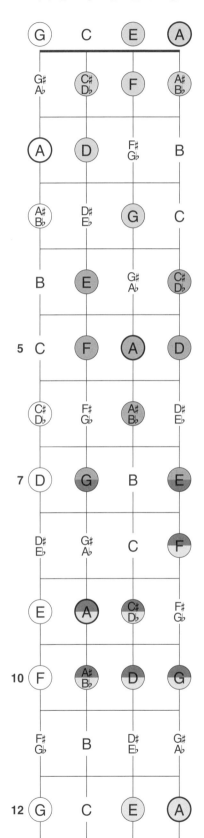

B♭ PHRYGIAN DOMINANT

B♭–C♭–D–E♭–F–G♭–A♭

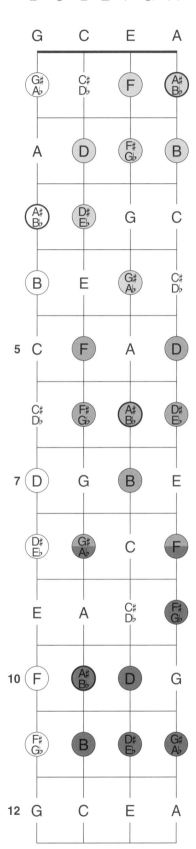

B PHRYGIAN DOMINANT

B–C–D♯–E–F♯–G–A

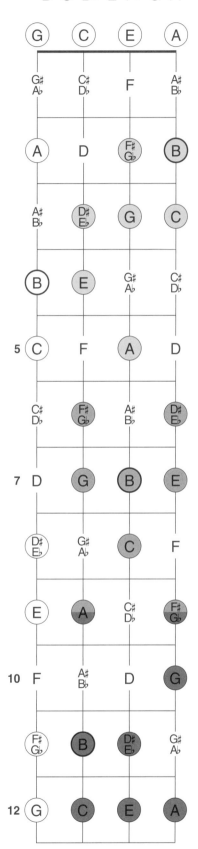

CHORDS
POWER CHORDS

C5

C–G

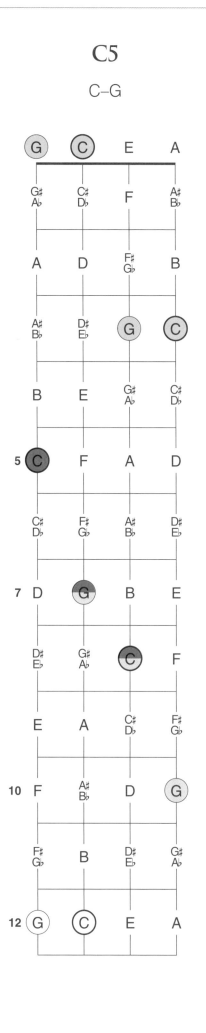

C#/Db5

C#–G#/Db–Ab

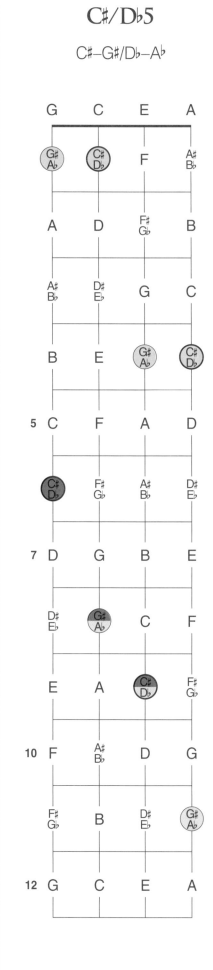

D5

D–A

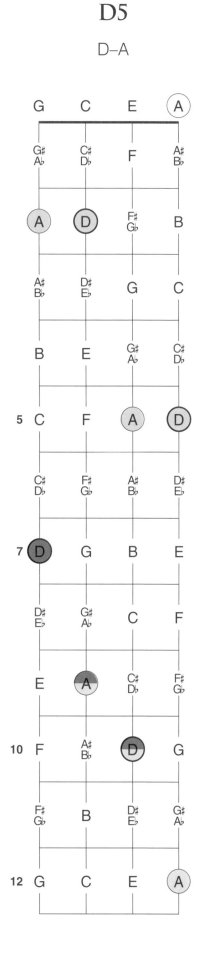

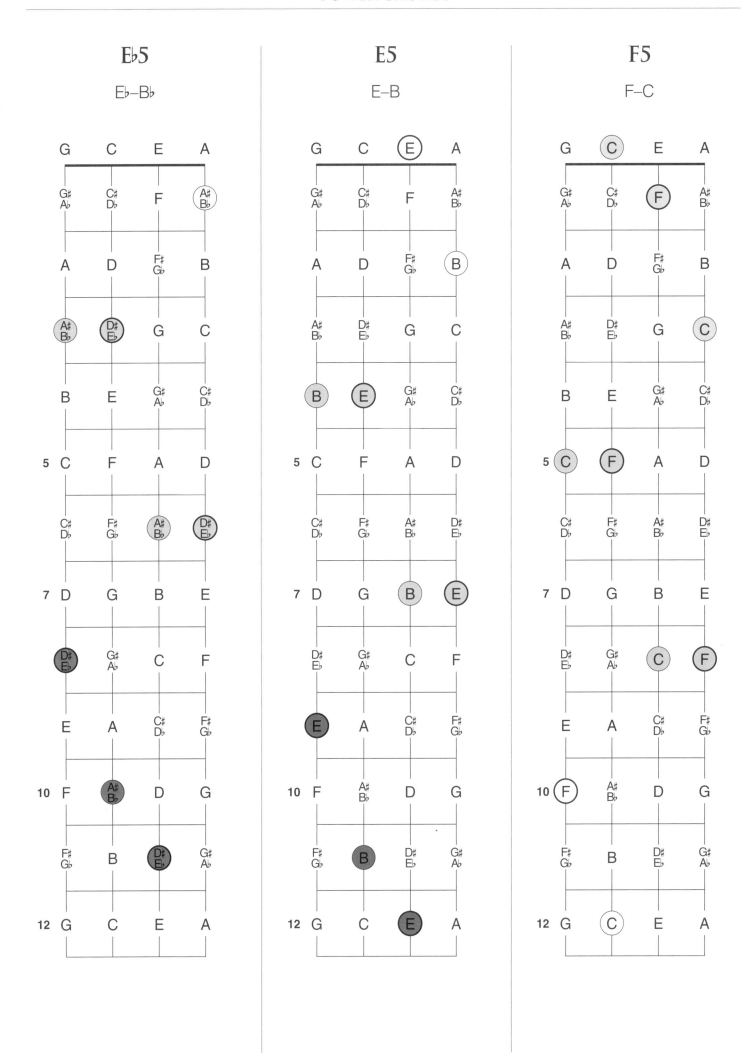

F#/Gb5

F#–C#/Gb–Db

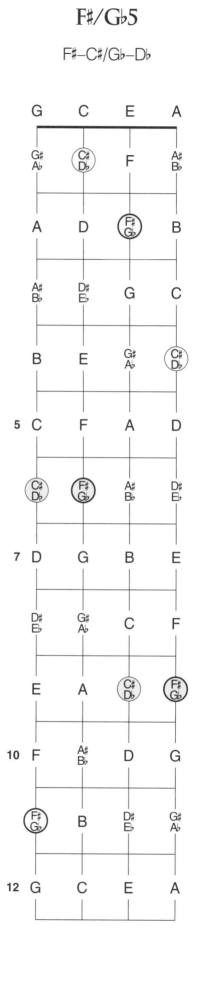

G5

G–D

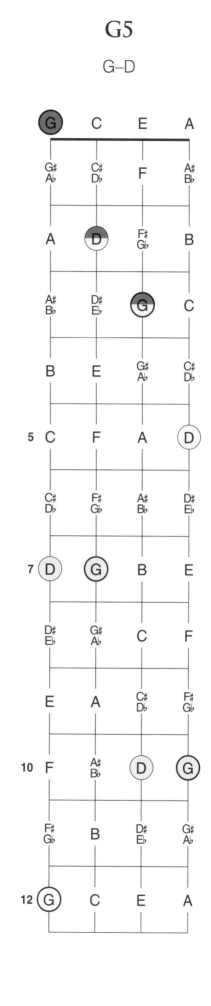

G#/Ab5

G#–D#/Ab–Eb

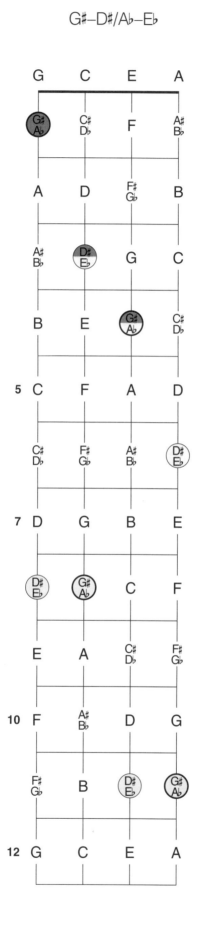

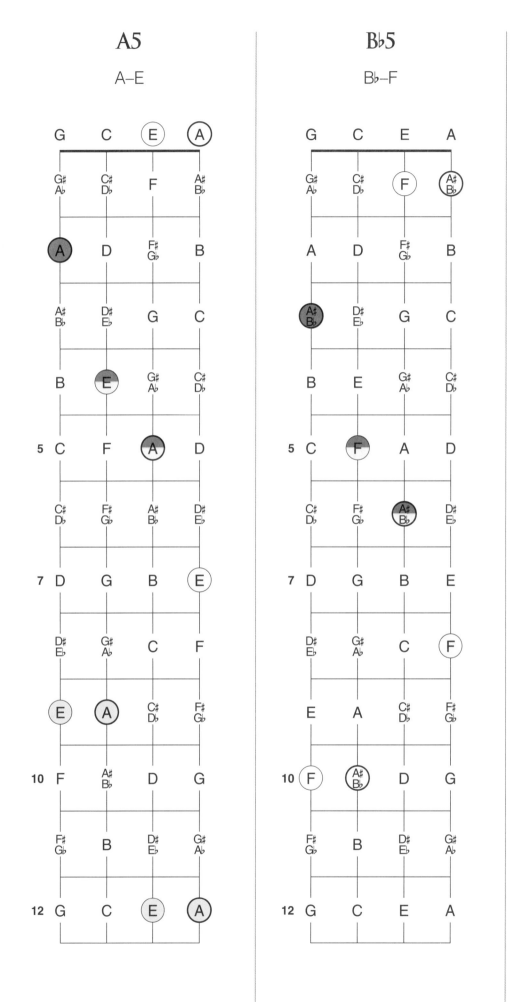

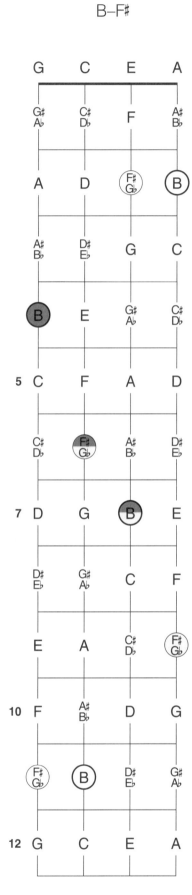

CHORDS
TRIADS

C

C–E–G

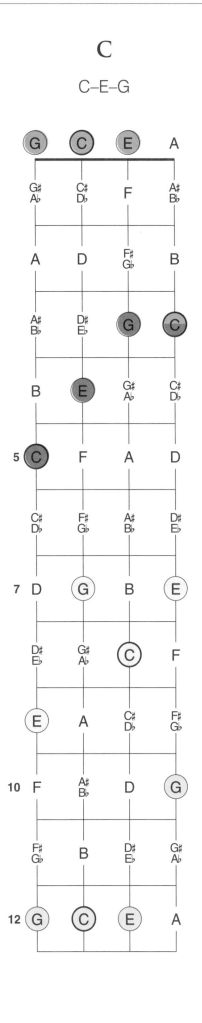

C♯/D♭

C♯–E♯–G♯/D♭–F–A♭

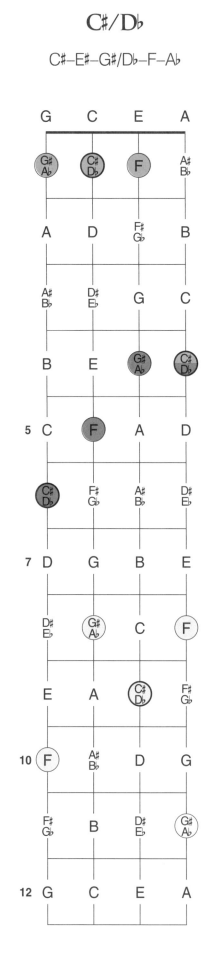

D

D–F♯–A

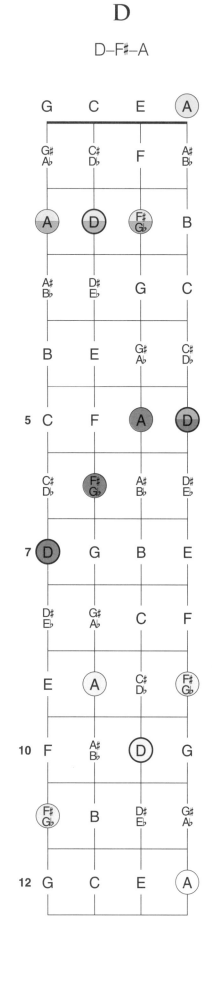

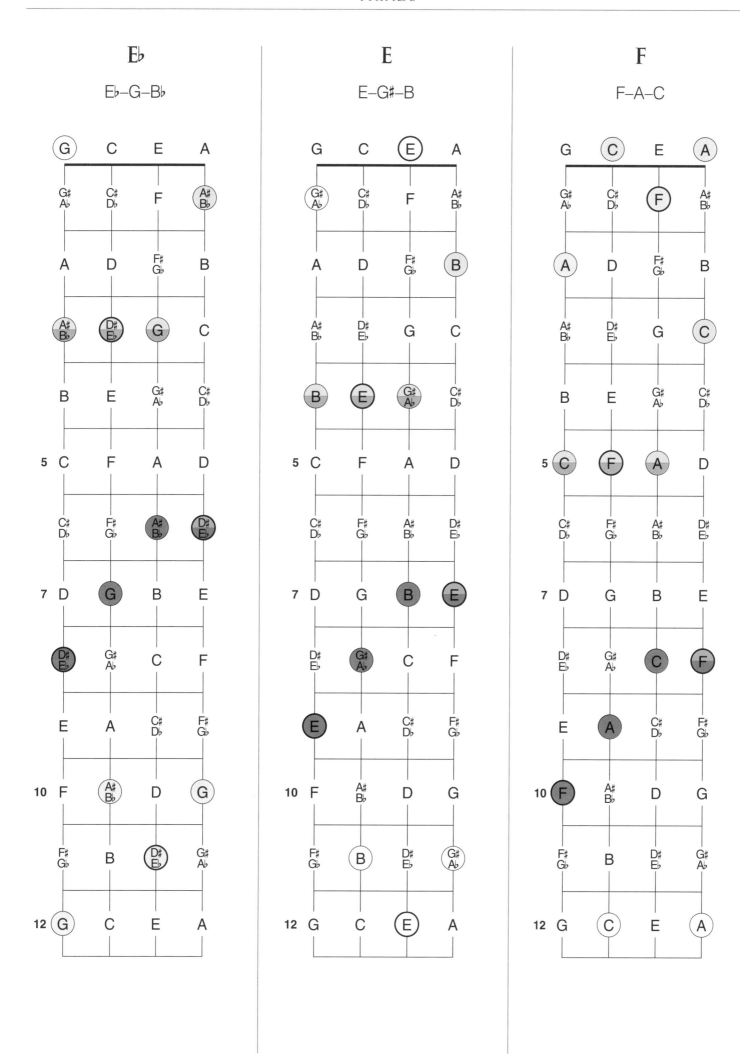

F#/G♭

F#–A#–C#/G♭–B♭–D♭

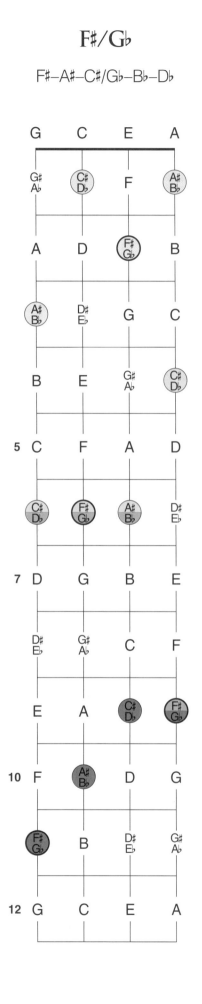

G

G–B–D

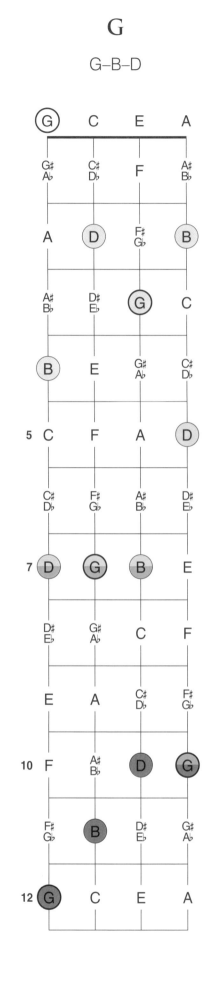

A♭

A♭–C–E♭

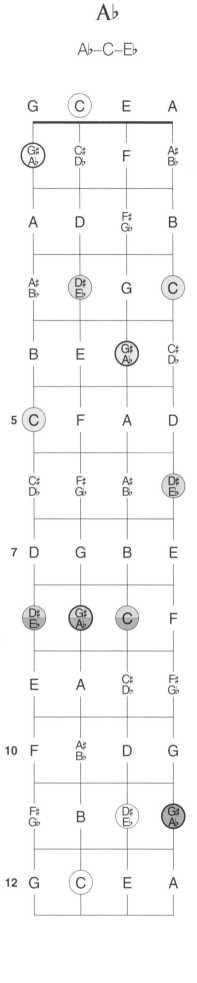

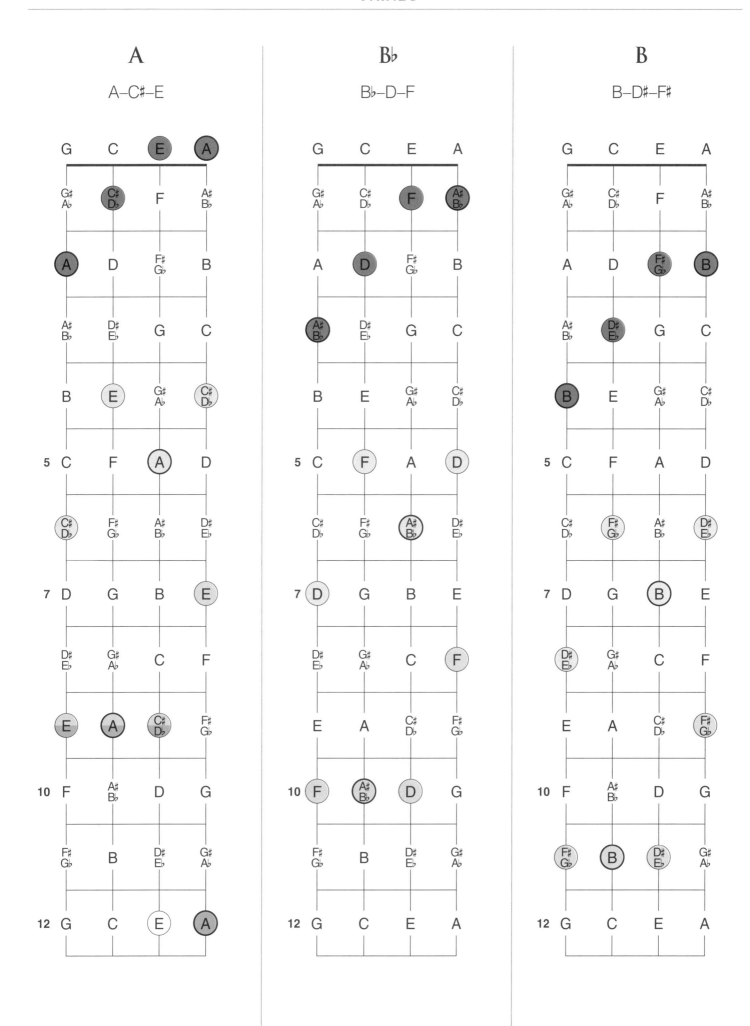

Csus4

C–F–G

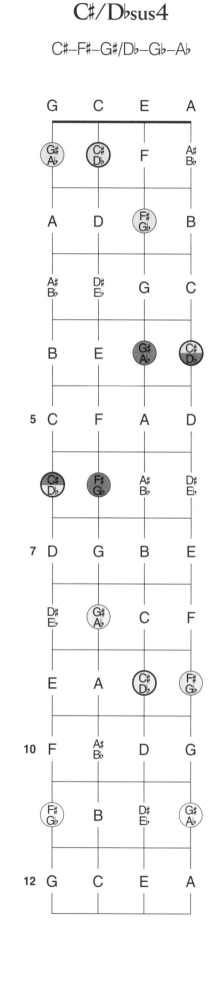

C#/D♭sus4

C#–F#–G#/D♭–G♭–A♭

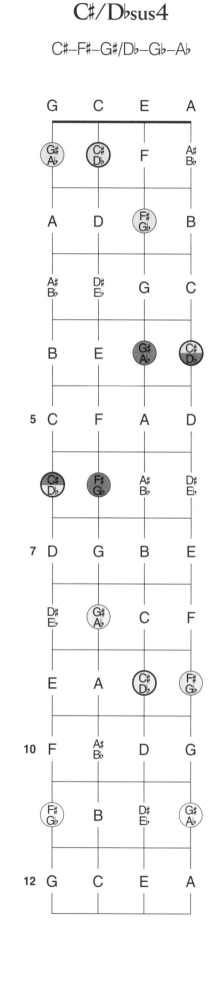

Dsus4

D–G–A

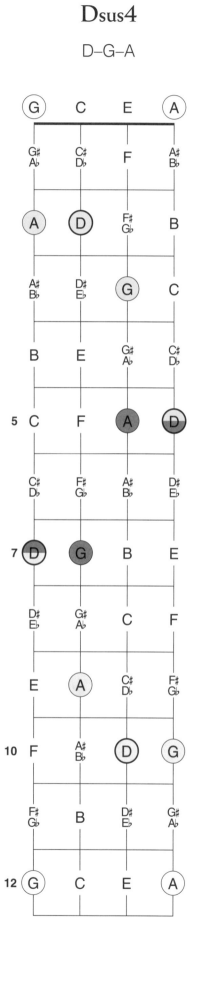

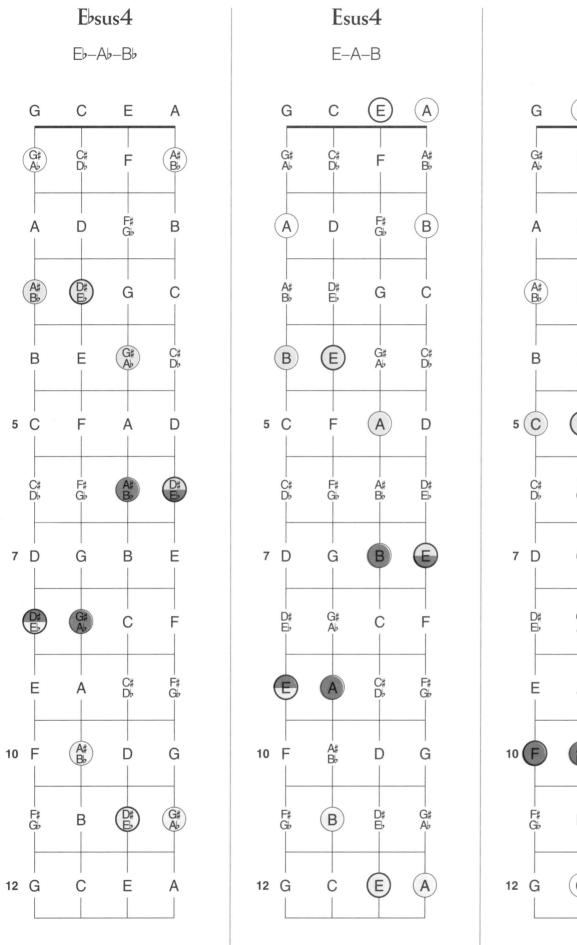
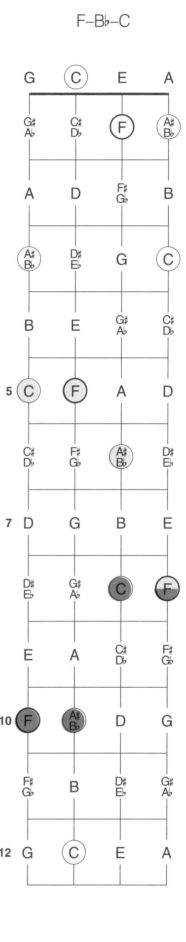

F#/G♭sus4

F#–B–C#/G♭–C♭–D♭

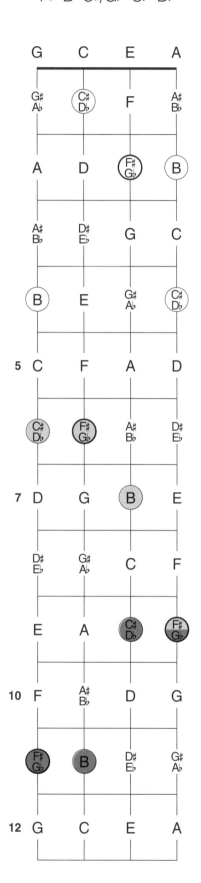

Gsus4

G–C–D

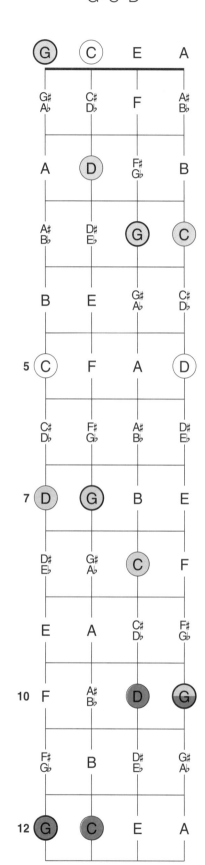

A♭sus4

A♭–D♭–E♭

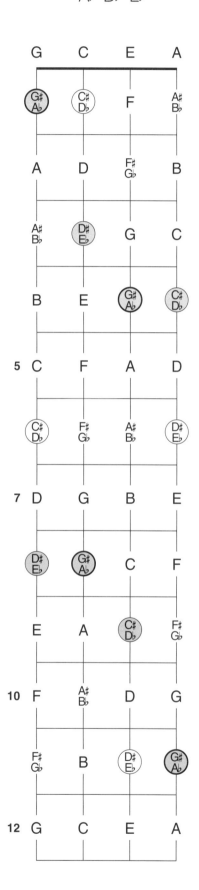

Asus4

A–D–E

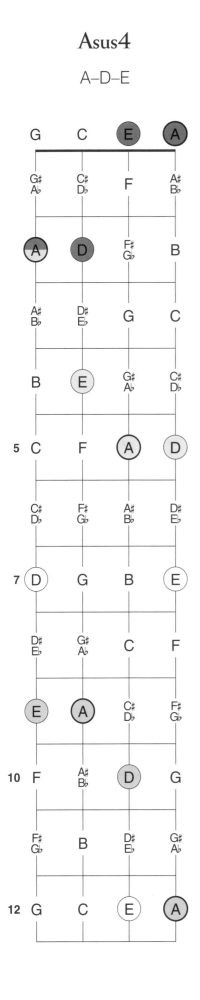

B♭sus4

B♭–E♭–F

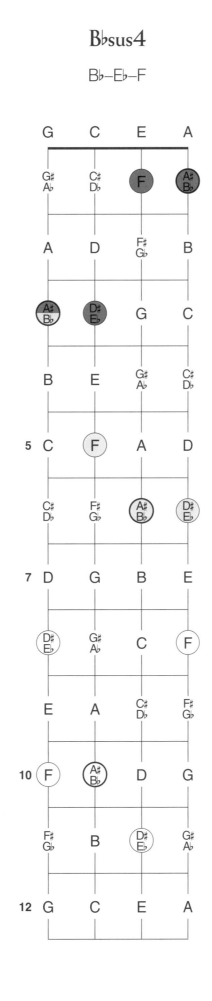

Bsus4

B–E–F♯

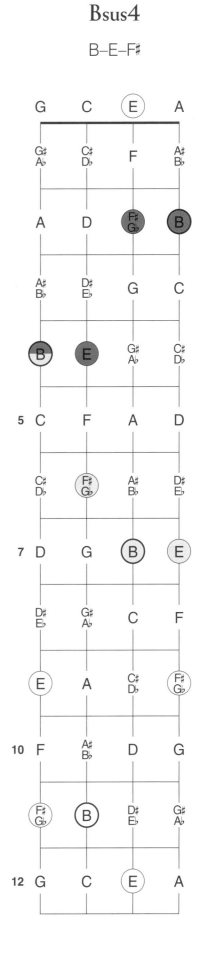

Cm

C–E♭–G

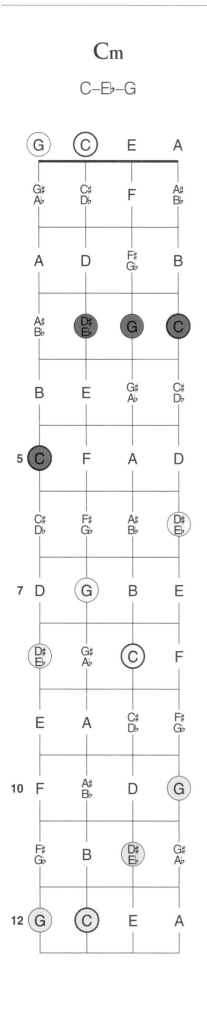

C♯m

C♯–E–G♯

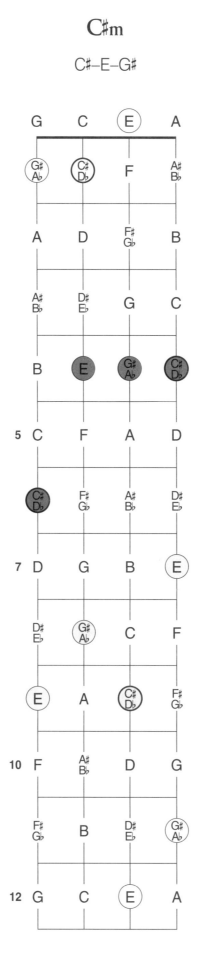

Dm

D–F–A

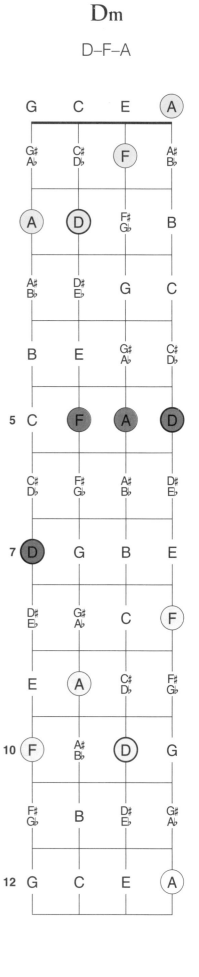

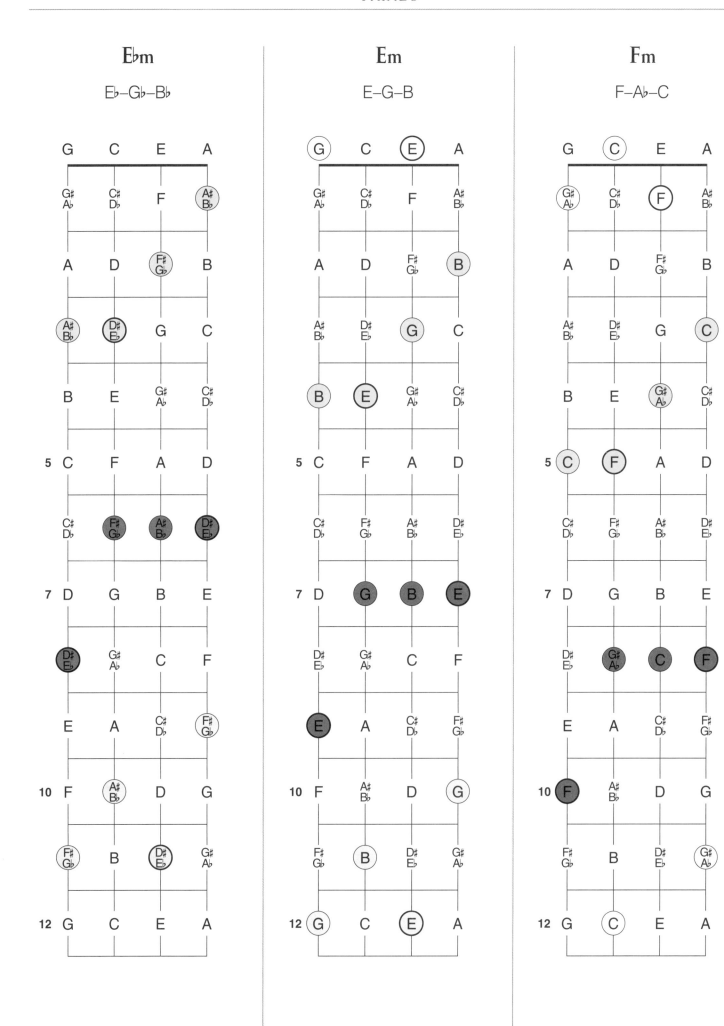

F#m

F#–A–C#

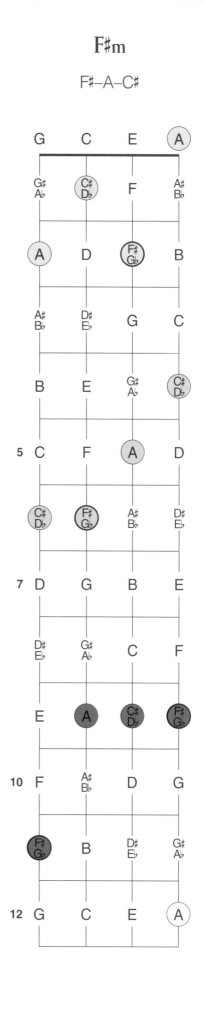

Gm

G–Bb–D

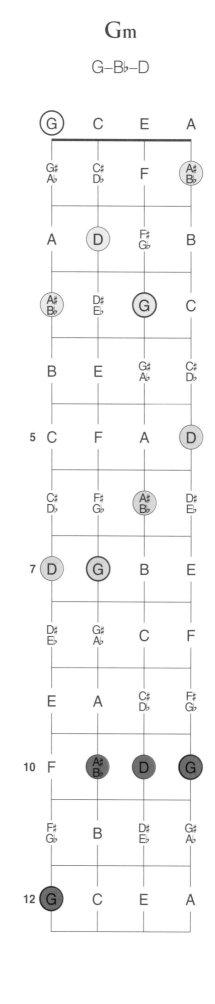

G#/Abm

G#–B–D#/Ab–Cb–Eb

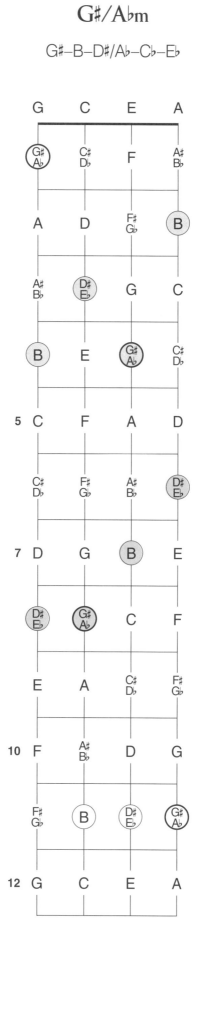

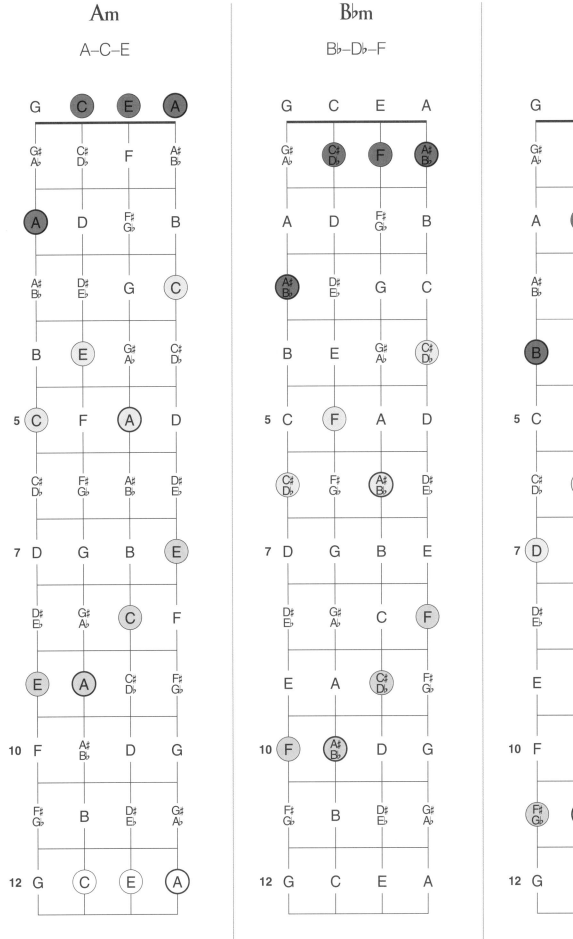

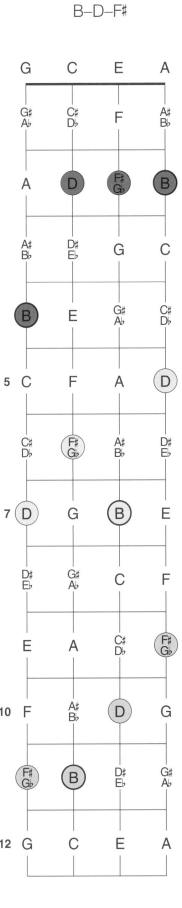

C+

C–E–G#

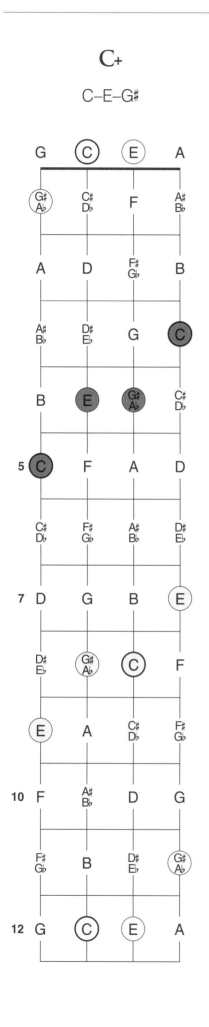

C#/D♭+

C#–E#–G×/D♭–F–A

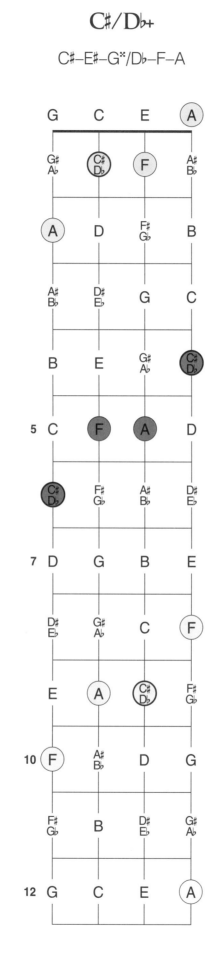

D+

D–F#–A#

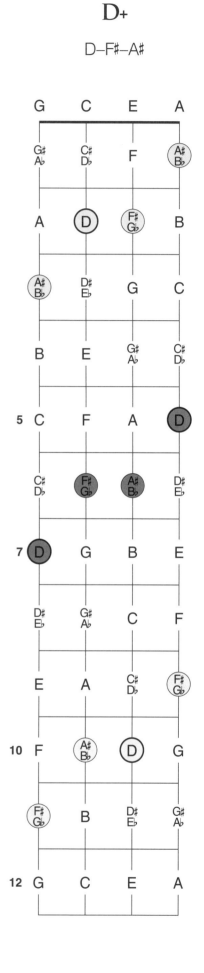

E♭+

E♭–G–B

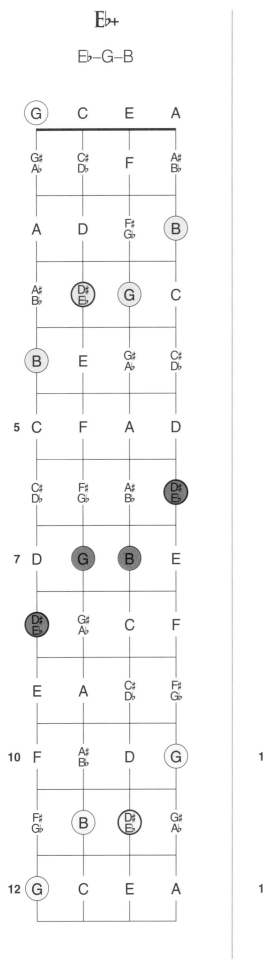

E+

E–G♯–B♯

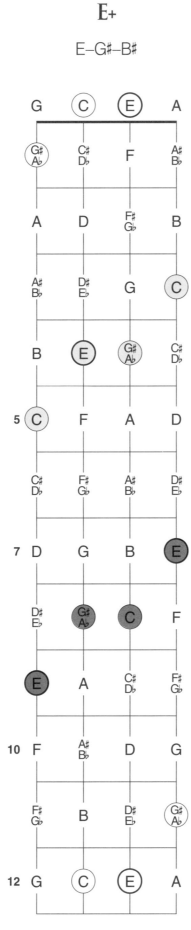

F+

F–A–C♯

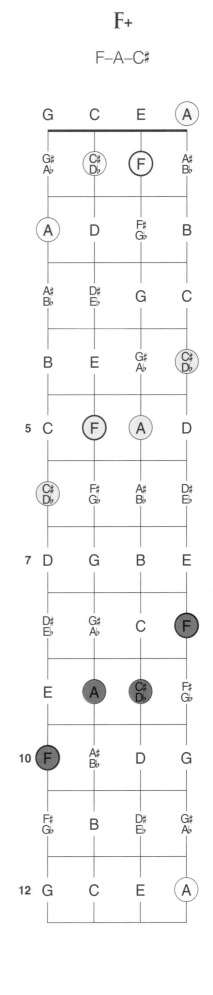

G♭+

G♭–B♭–D

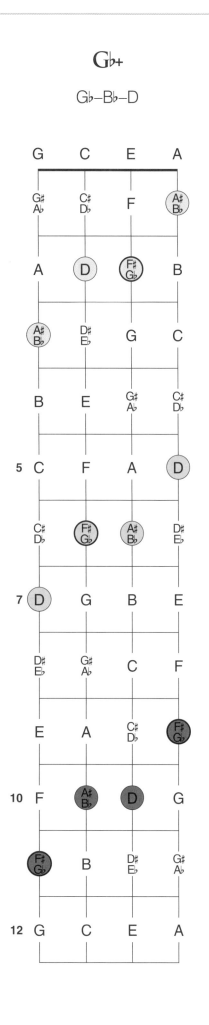

G+

G–B–D♯

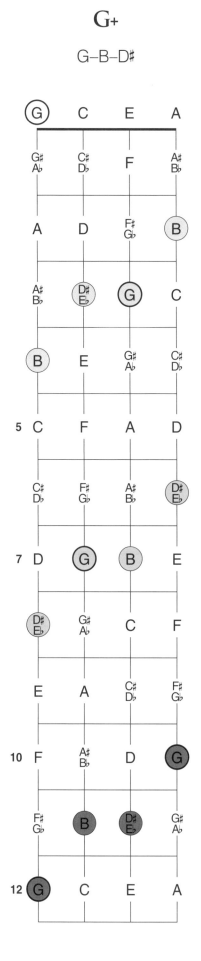

A♭+

A♭–C–E

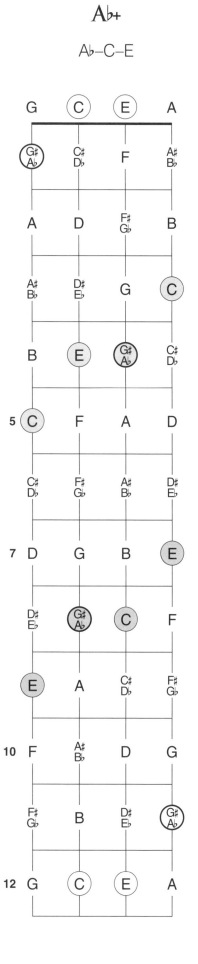

A+

A–C#–E#

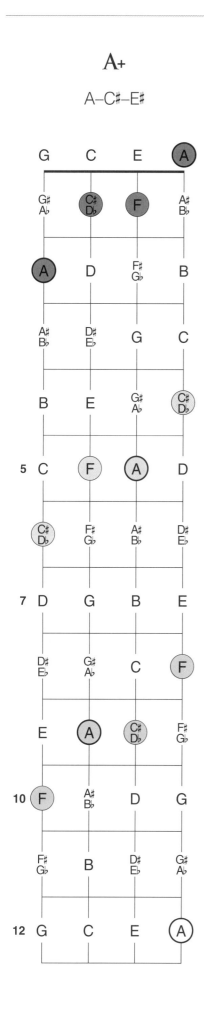

Bb+

Bb–D–F#

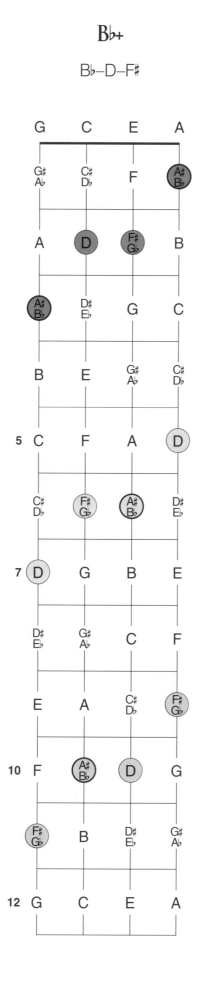

B+

B–D#–G

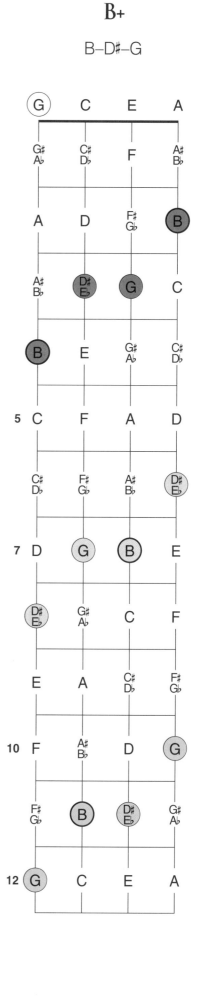

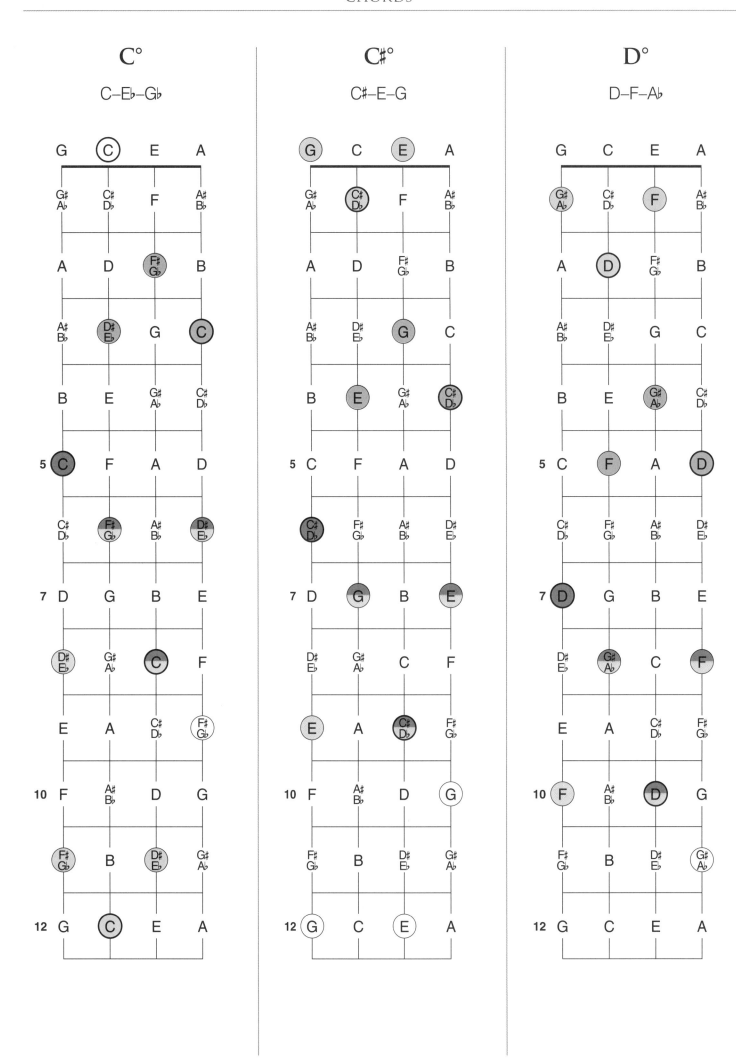

D#°

D#–F#–A

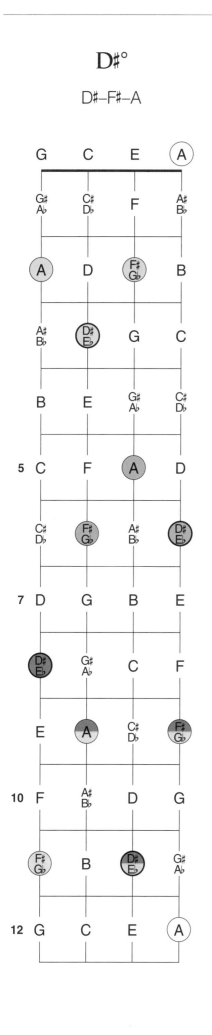

E°

E–G–B♭

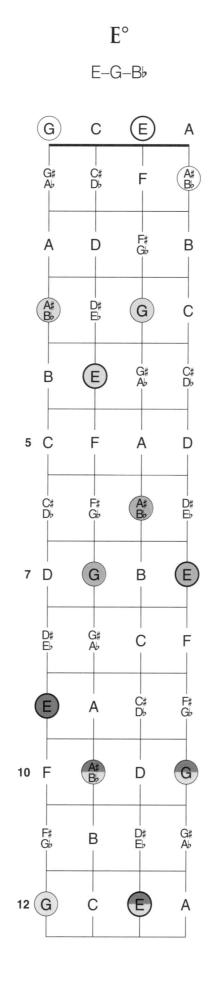

F°

F–A♭–C♭

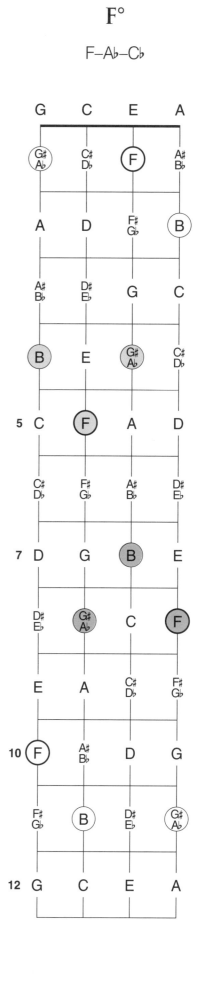

F#°

F#–A–C

G°

G–Bb–Db

G#°

G#–B–D

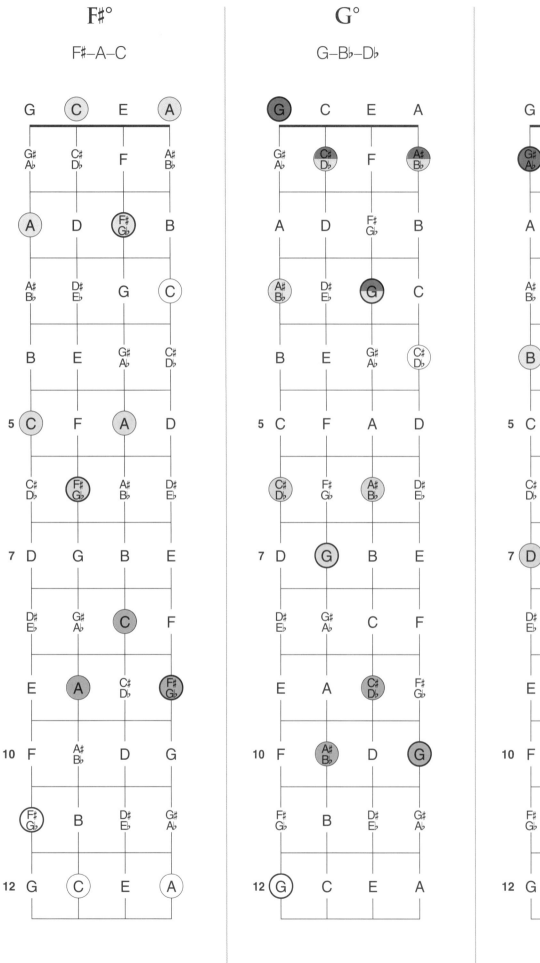
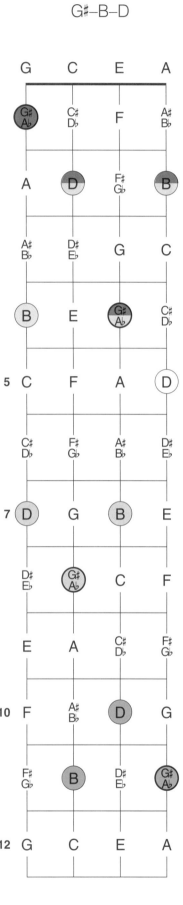

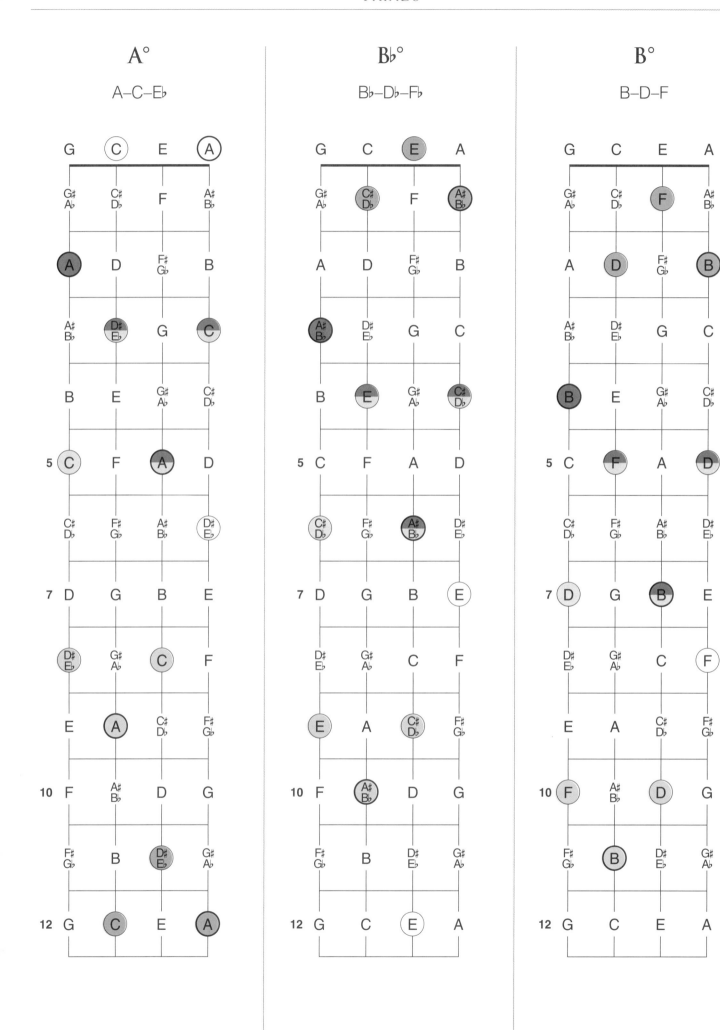

CHORDS

TRIADS WITH ADDED NOTES

Cadd9

C–E–G–D

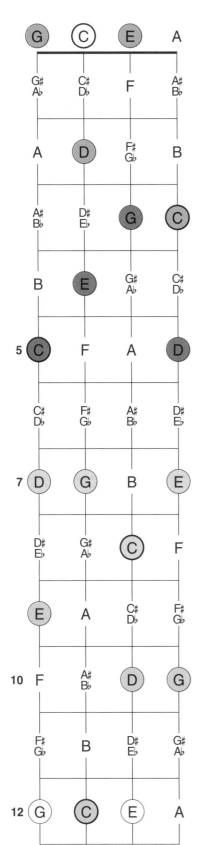

C♯/D♭add9

C♯–E♯–G♯–D♯/D♭–F–A♭–E♭

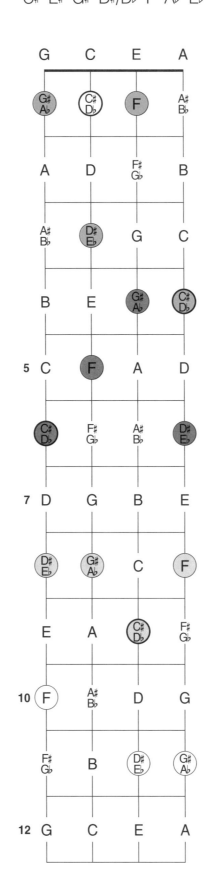

Dadd9

D–F♯–A–E

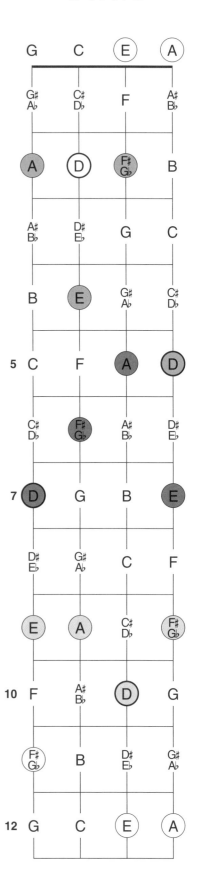

E♭add9

E♭–G–B♭–F

Eadd9

E–G#–B–F#

Fadd9

F–A–C–G

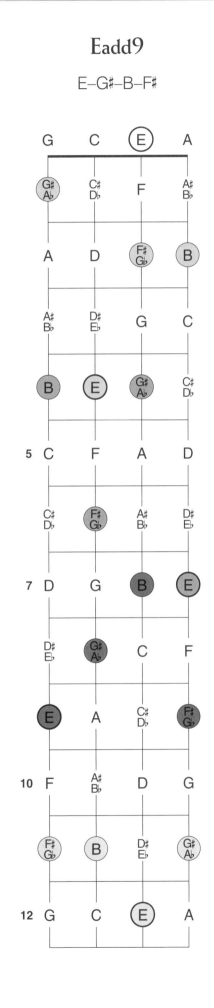

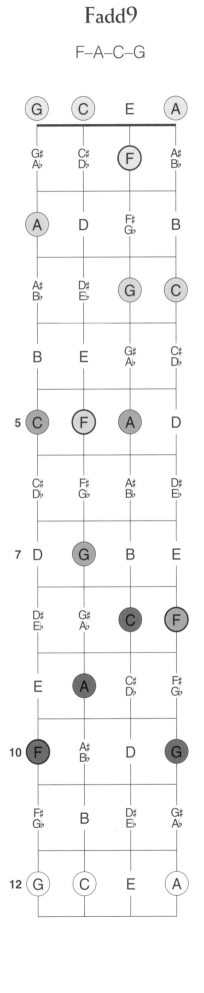

F#/G♭add9

F#–A#–C#–G#/G♭–B♭–D♭–A♭

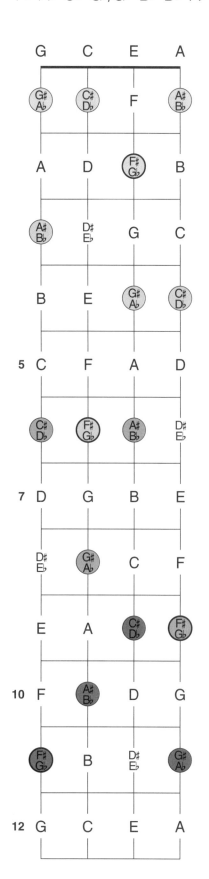

Gadd9

G–B–D–A

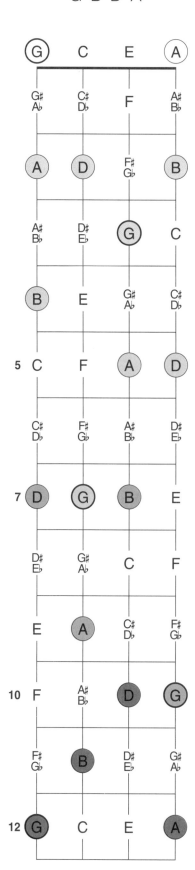

A♭add9

A♭–C–E♭–B♭

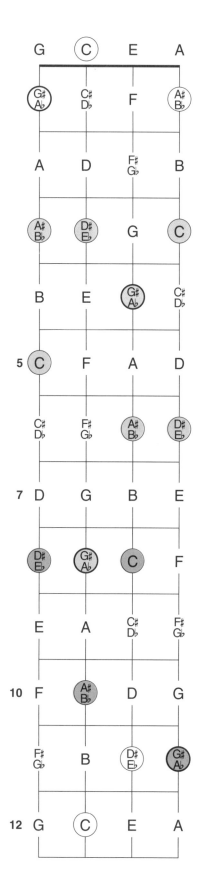

Aadd9

A–C#–E–B

B♭add9

B♭–D–F–C

Badd9

B–D#–F#–C#

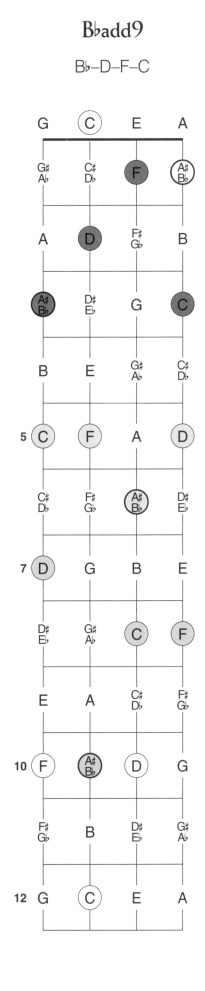
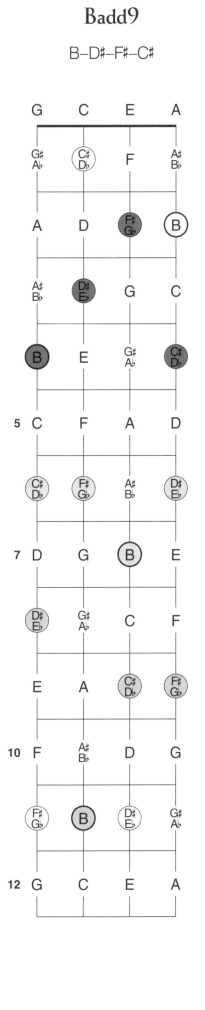

Cm(add9)

C–E♭–G–D

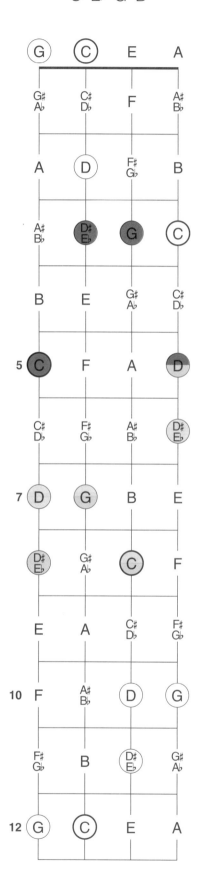

C#m(add9)

C#–E–G#–D#

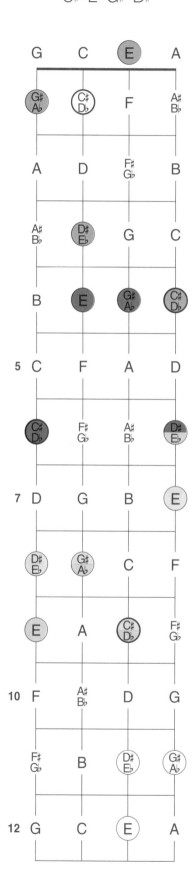

Dm(add9)

D–F–A–E

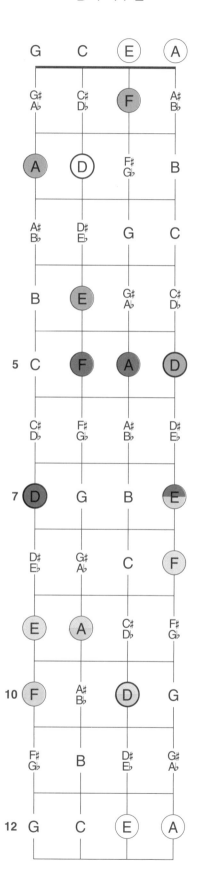

E♭m(add9)

E♭–G♭–B♭–F

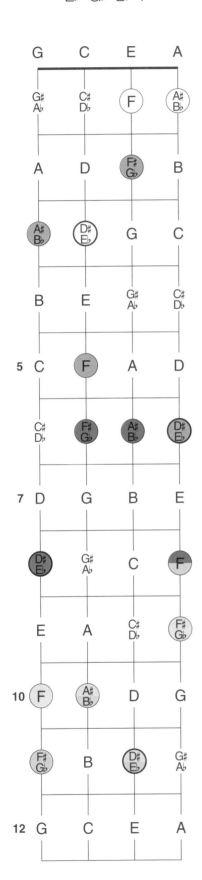

Em(add9)

E–G–B–F♯

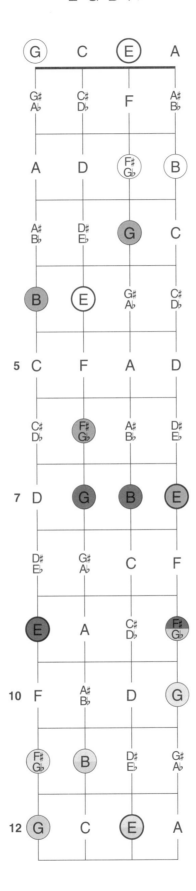

Fm(add9)

F–A♭–C–G

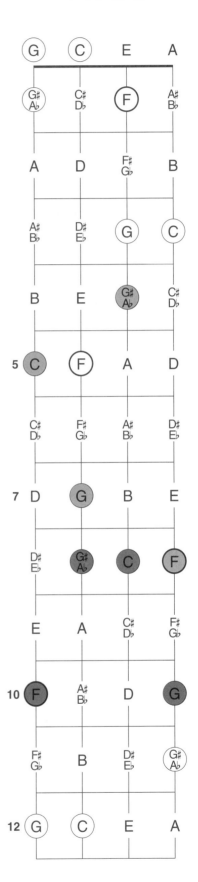

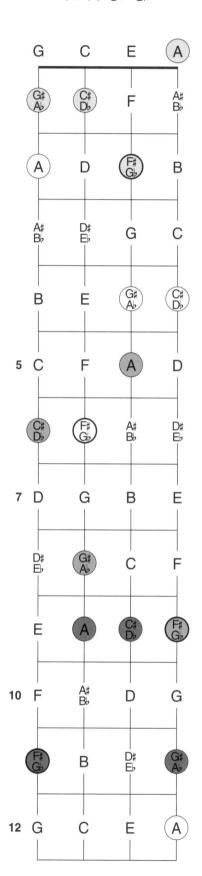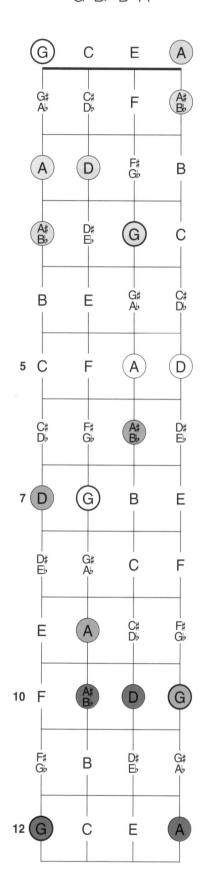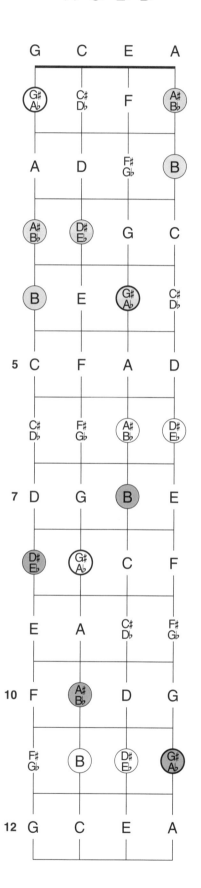

F#m(add9)

F#–A–C#–G#

Gm(add9)

G–B♭–D–A

A♭m(add9)

A♭–C♭–E♭–B♭

Am(add9)

A–C–E–B

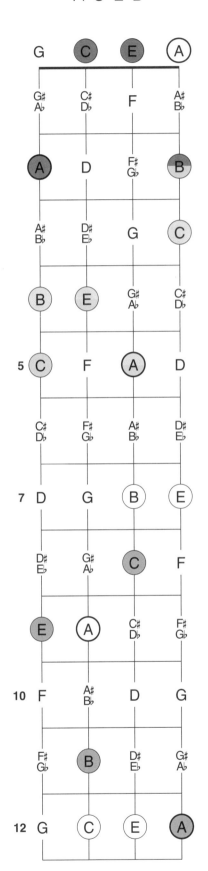

B♭m(add9)

B♭–D♭–F–C

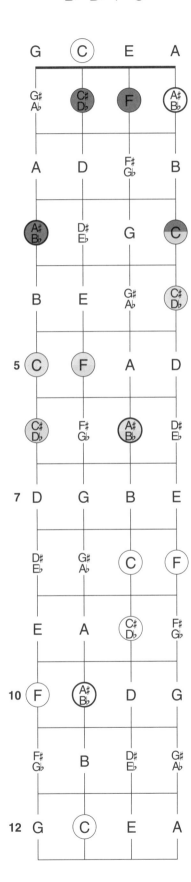

Bm(add9)

B–D–F♯–C♯

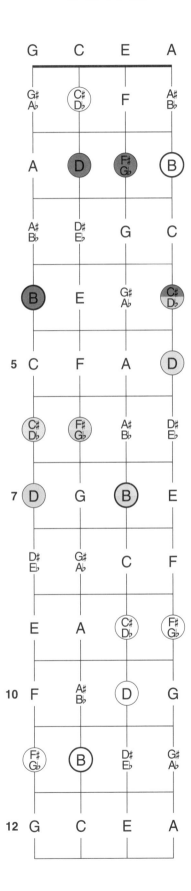

C6

C–E–G–A

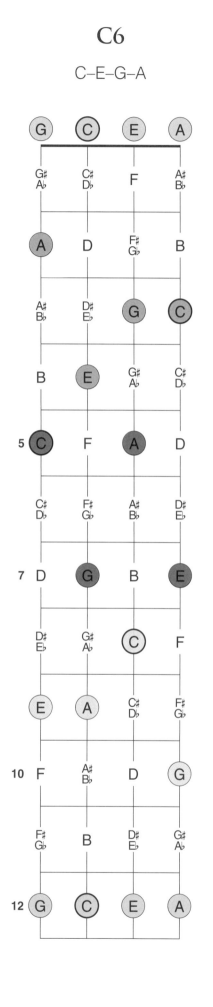

C#/D♭6

C#–E#–G#–A#/D♭–F–A♭–B♭

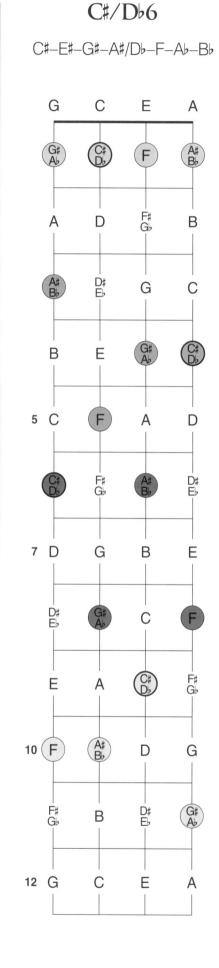

D6

D–F#–A–B

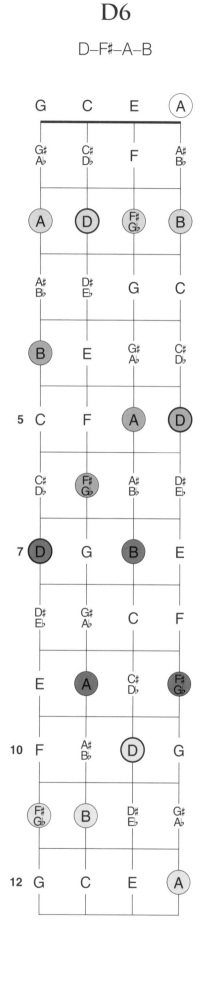

E♭6

E♭–G–B♭–C

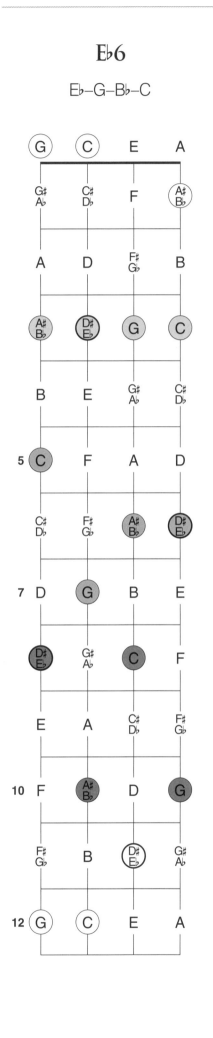

E6

E–G#–B–C#

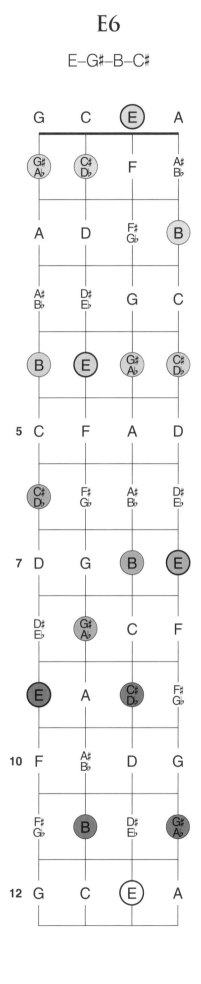

F6

F–A–C–D

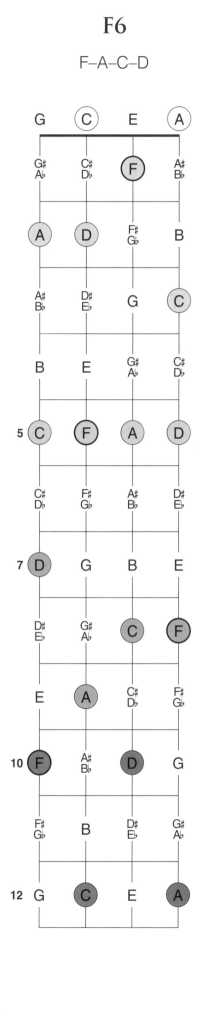

F#/G♭6

F#–A#–C#–D#/G♭–B♭–D♭–E♭

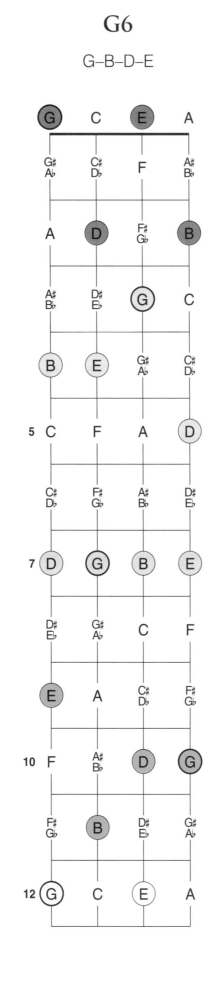

G6

G–B–D–E

A♭6

A♭–C–E♭–F

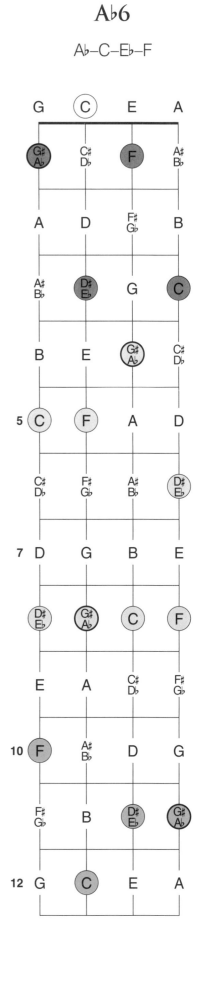

A6

A–C#–E–F#

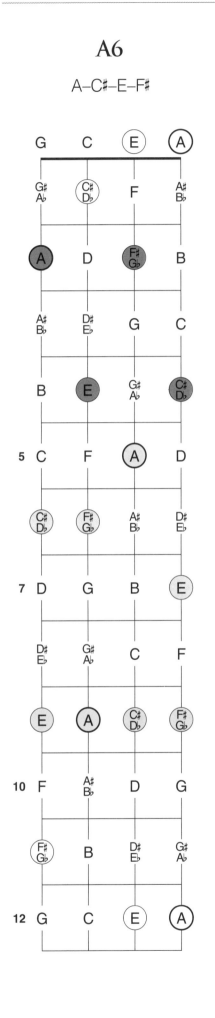

B♭6

B♭–D–F–G

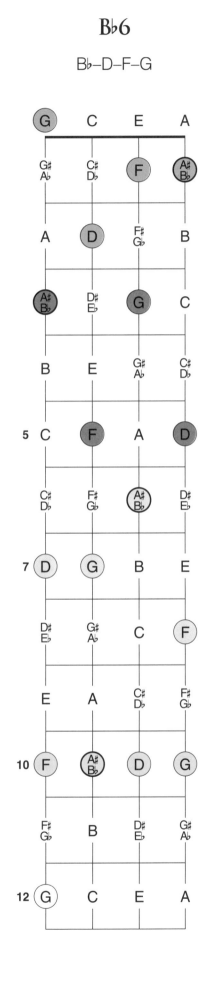

B6

B–D#–F#–G#

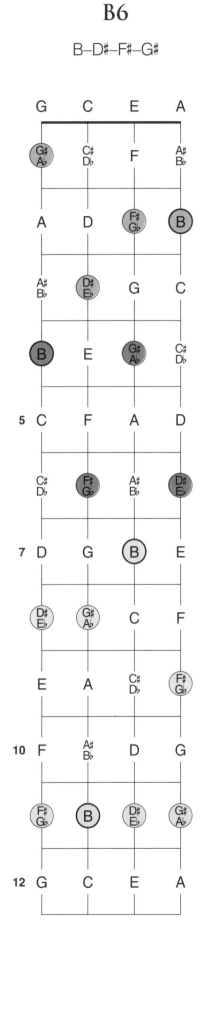

Cm6

C–E♭–G–A

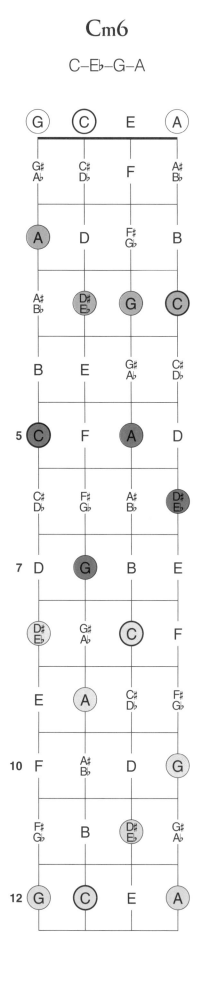

C♯m6

C♯–E–G♯–A♯

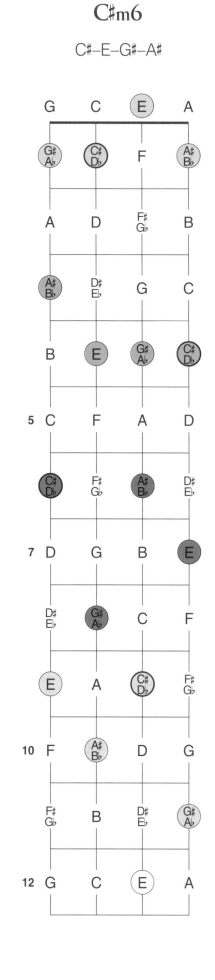

Dm6

D–F–A–B

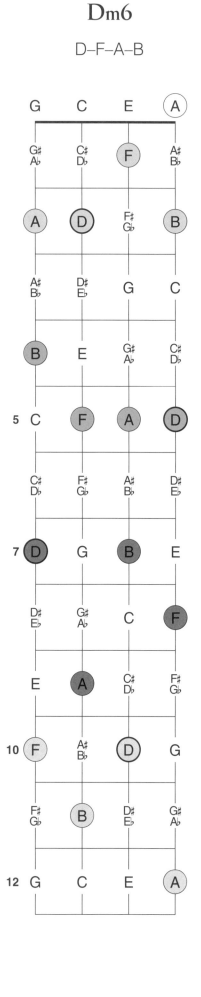

E♭m6

E♭–G♭–B♭–C

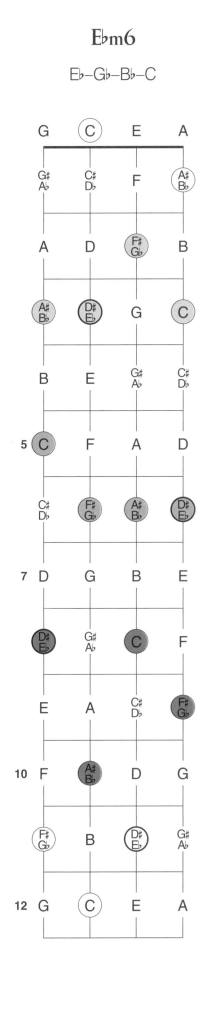

Em6

E–G–B–C♯

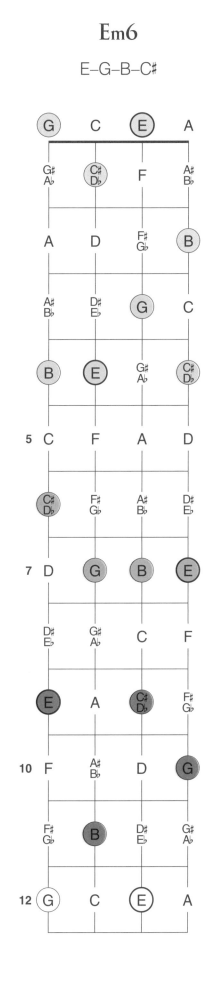

Fm6

F–A♭–C–D

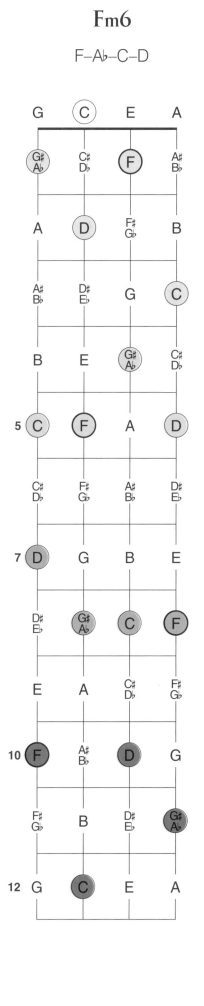

F#m6

F#–A–C#–D#

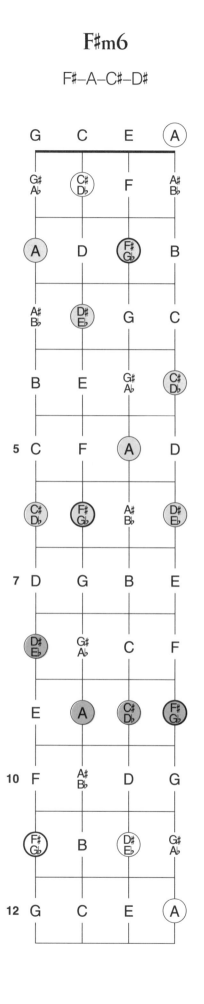

Gm6

G–Bb–D–E

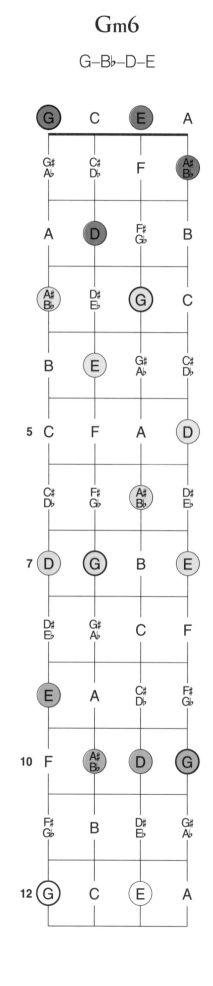

Abm6

Ab–Cb–Eb–F

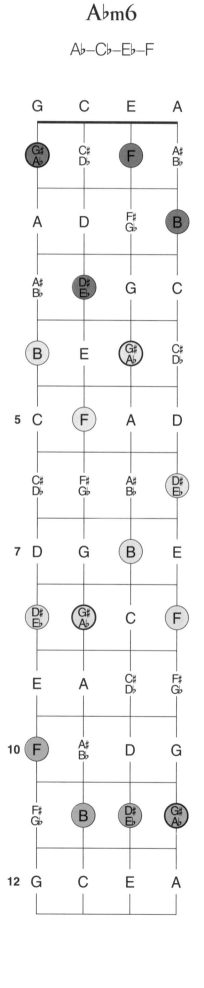

Am6

A–C–E–F#

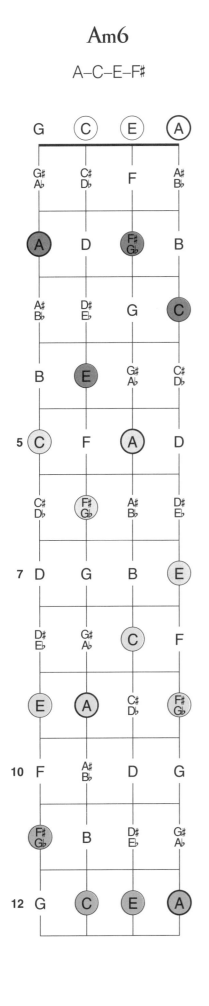

B♭m6

B♭–D♭–F–G

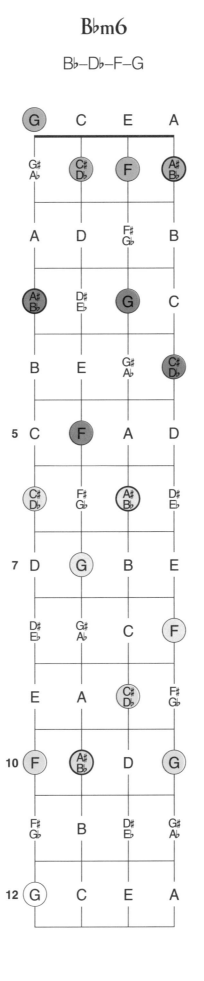

Bm6

B–D–F#–G#

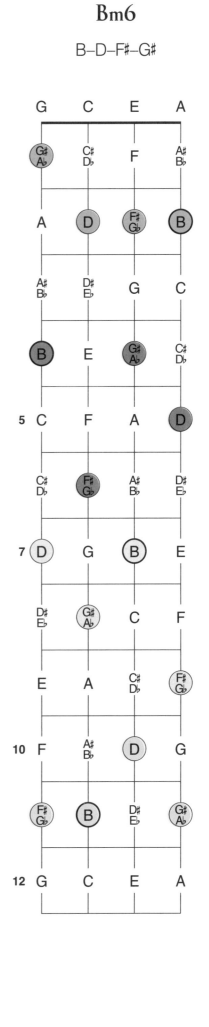

C^6_9

C–E–G–A–D

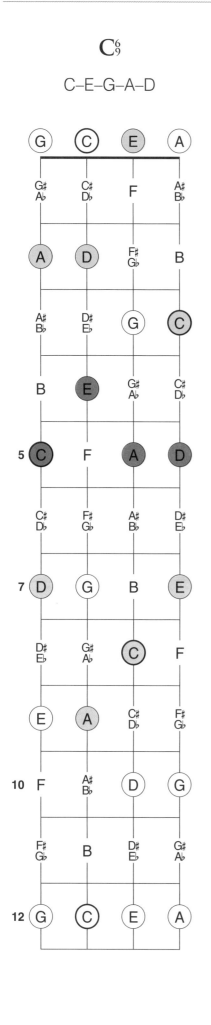

$C\sharp/D\flat^6_9$

C#–E#–G#–A#–D#/D♭–F–A♭–B♭–E♭

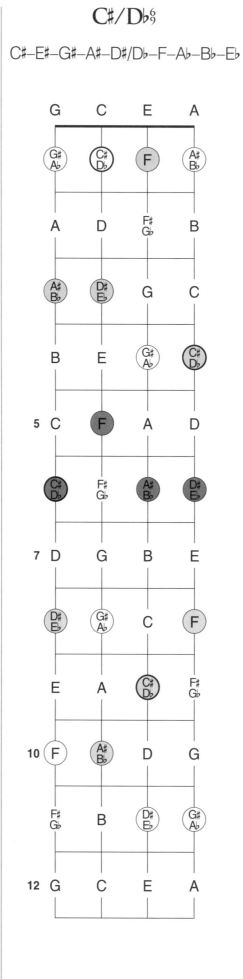

D^6_9

D–F#–A–B–E

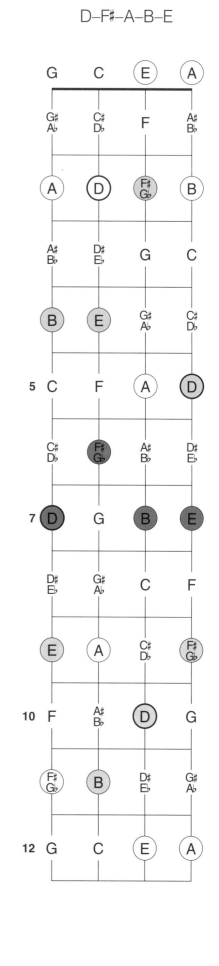

E♭⁶₉

E♭–G–B♭–C–F

E⁶₉

E–G#–B–C#–F#

F⁶₉

F–A–C–D–G

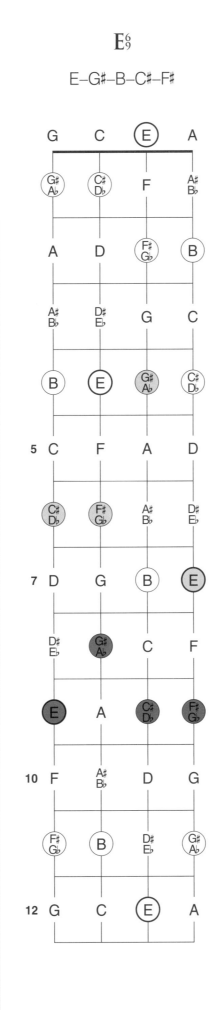

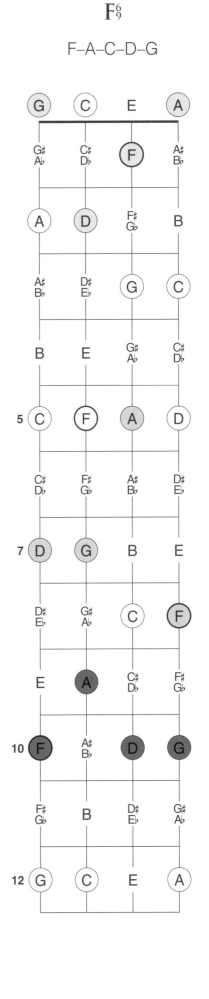

F#/G♭$^6_9$

F#–A#–C#–D#–G#/G♭–B♭–D♭–E♭–A♭

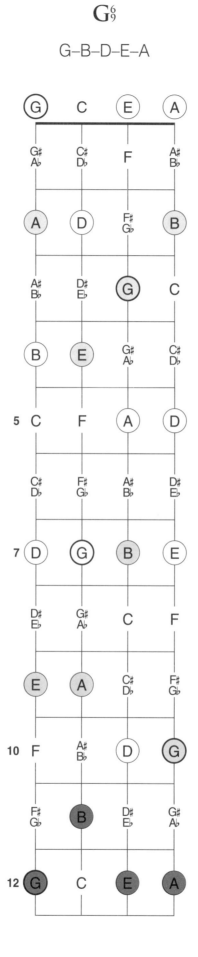

G$^6_9$

G–B–D–E–A

A♭$^6_9$

A♭–C–E♭–F–B♭

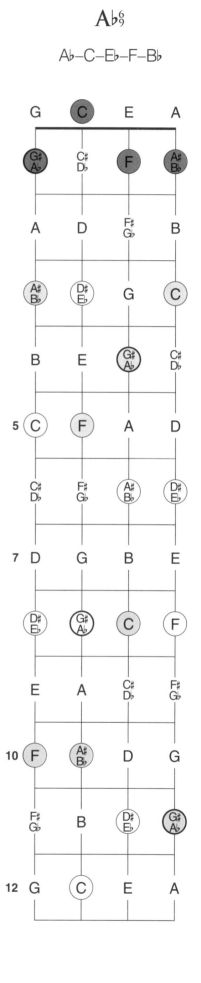

A^6_9

A–C#–E–F#–B

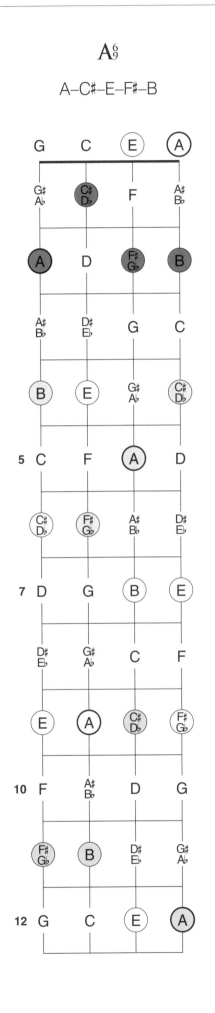

$B\flat^6_9$

B♭–D–F–G–C

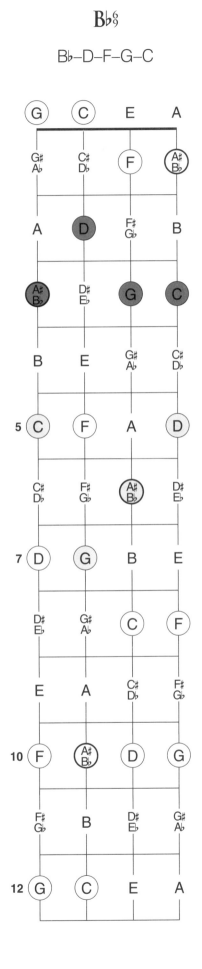

B^6_9

B–D#–F#–G#–C#

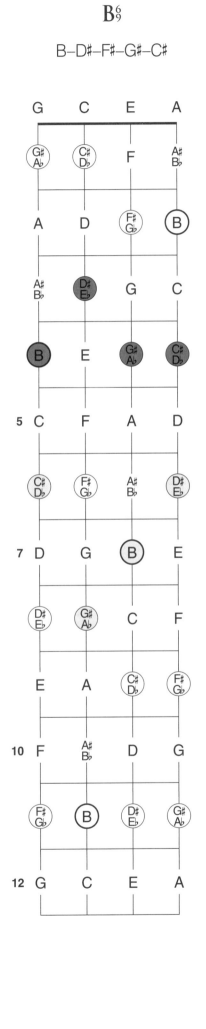

Cm⁶₉

C–E♭–G–A–D

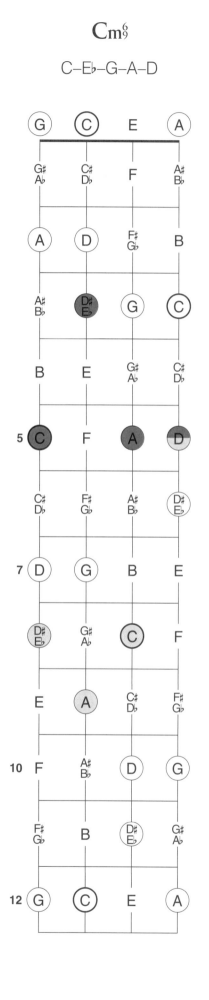

C#m⁶₉

C#–E–G#–A#–D#

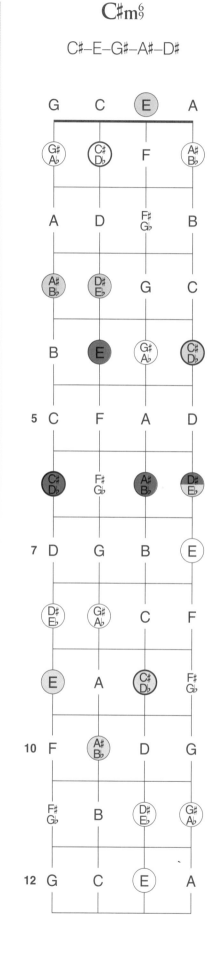

Dm⁶₉

D–F–A–B–E

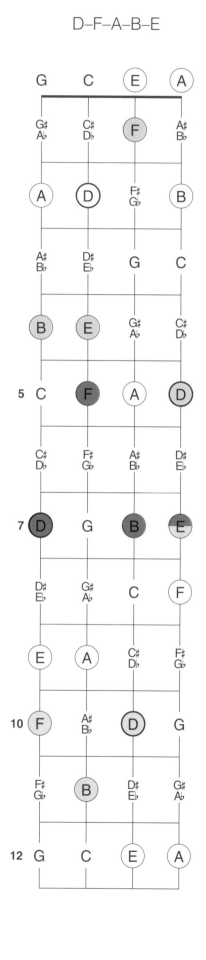

E♭m⁶₉

E♭–G♭–B♭–C–F

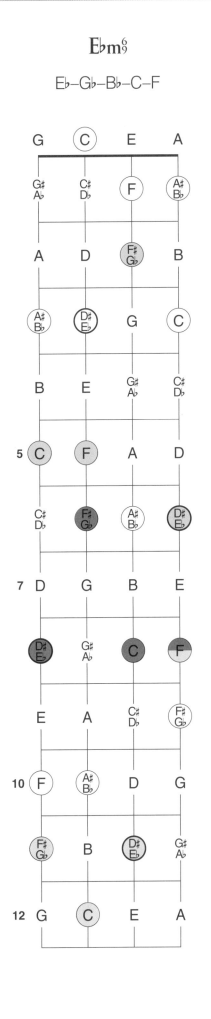

Em⁶₉

E–G–B–C♯–F♯

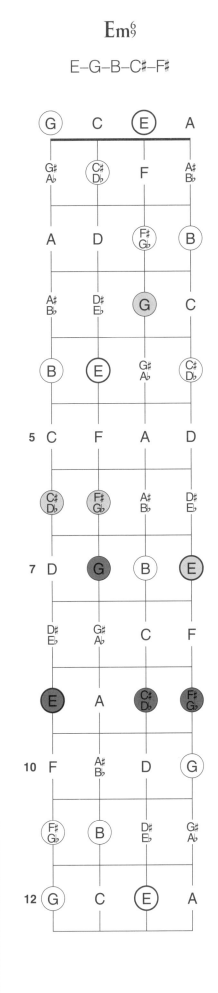

Fm⁶₉

F–A♭–C–D–G

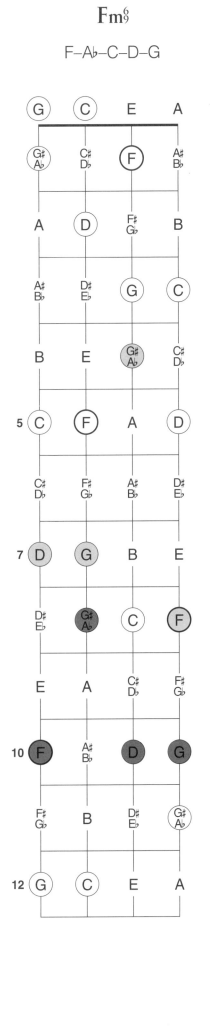

F#m⁶₉

F#–A–C#–D#–G#

Gm⁶₉

G–B♭–D–E–A

A♭m⁶₉

A♭–C♭–E♭–F–B♭

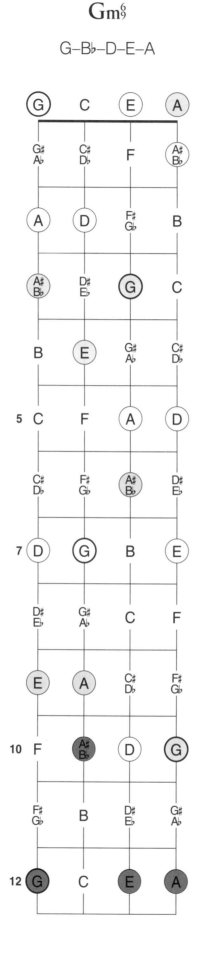
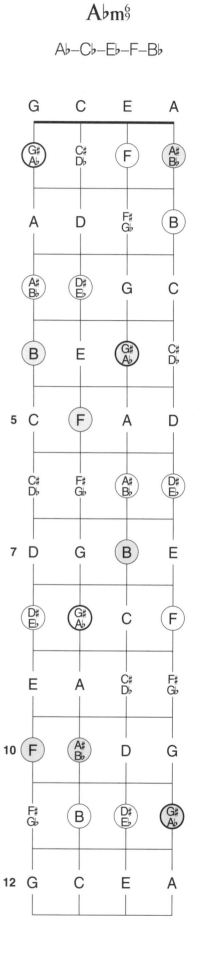

Am⁶/₉

A–C–E–F#–B

B♭m⁶/₉

B♭–D♭–F–G–C

Bm⁶/₉

B–D–F#–G#–C#

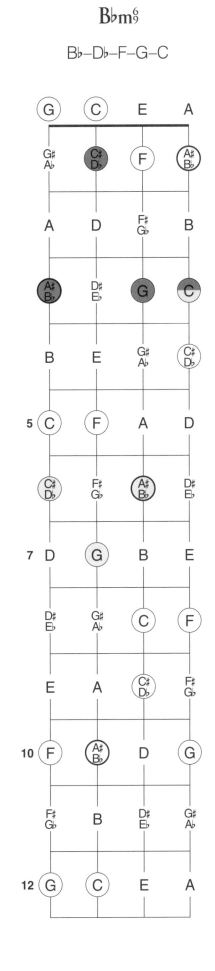

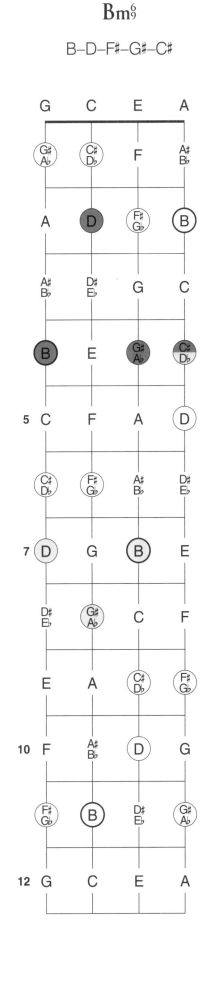

CHORDS
SEVENTH CHORDS

Cmaj7

C–E–G–B

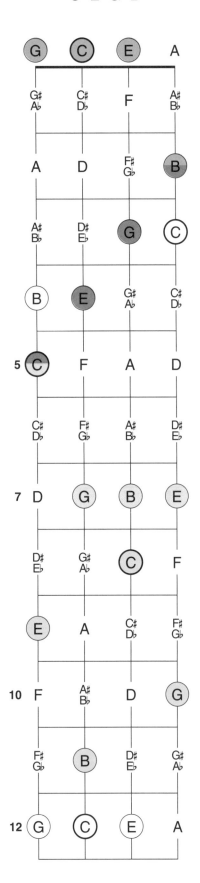

C♯/D♭maj7

C♯–E♯–G♯–B♯/D♭–F–A♭–C

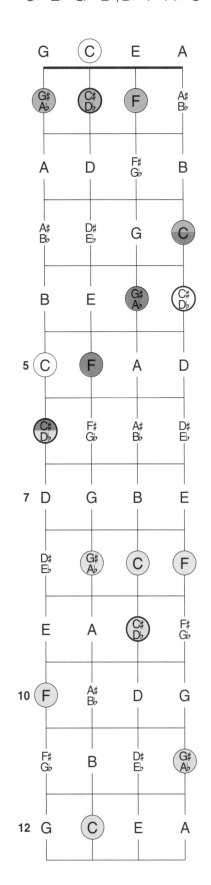

Dmaj7

D–F♯–A–C♯

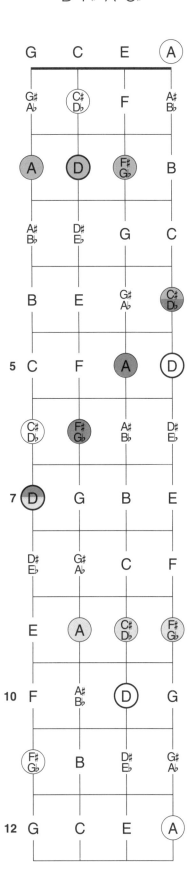

E♭maj7

E♭–G–B♭–D

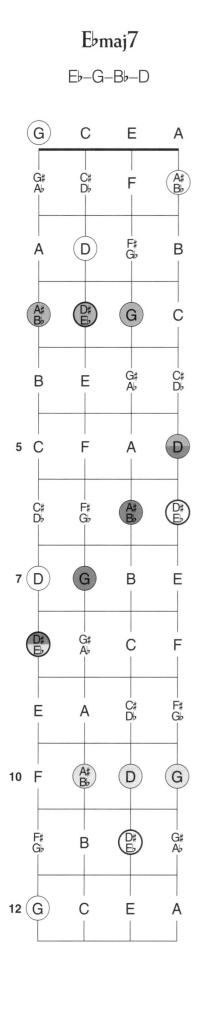

Emaj7

E–G#–B–D#

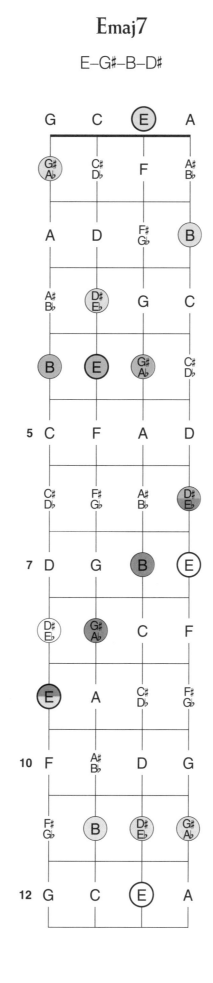

Fmaj7

F–A–C–E

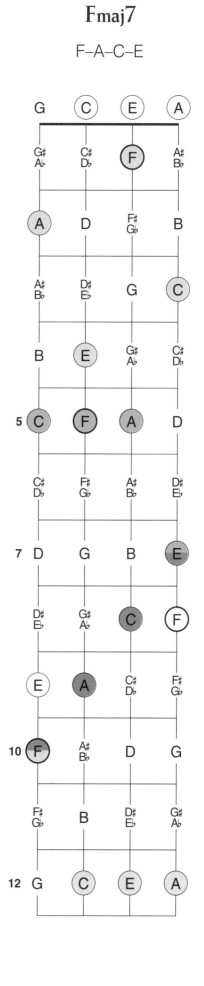

F♯/G♭maj7

F♯–A♯–C♯–E♯/G♭–B♭–D♭–F

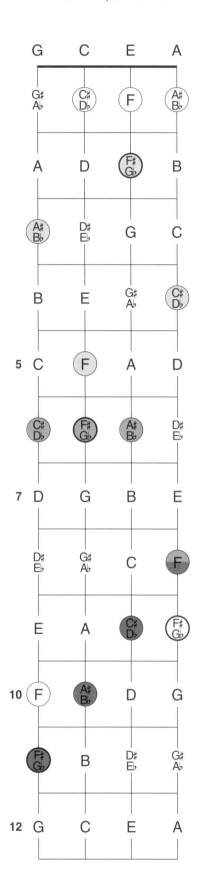

Gmaj7

G–B–D–F♯

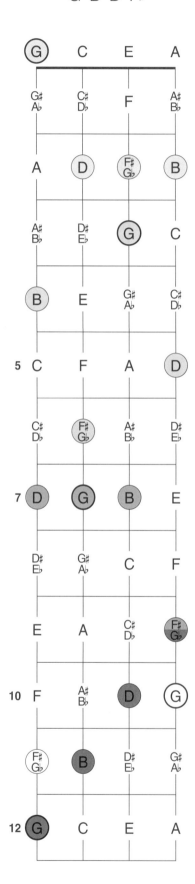

A♭maj7

A♭–C–E♭–G

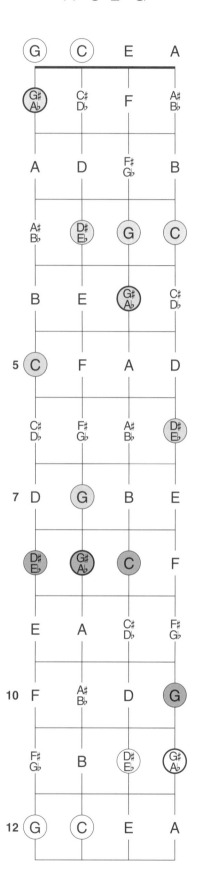

Amaj7

A–C#–E–G#

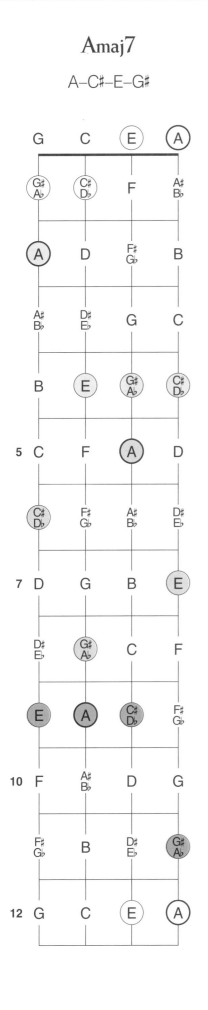

B♭maj7

B♭–D–F–A

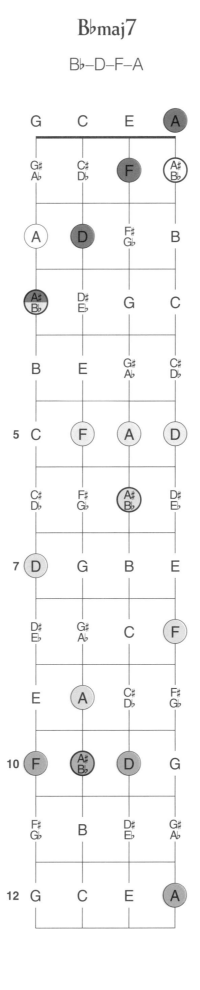

Bmaj7

B–D#–F#–A#

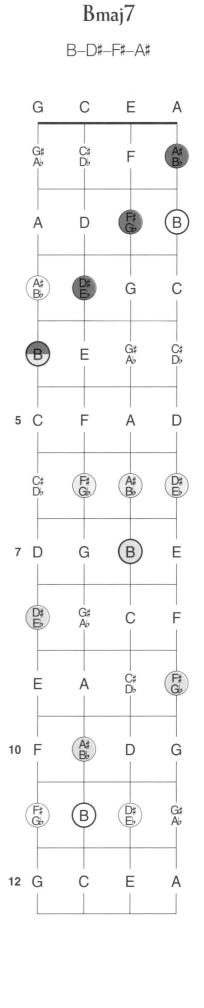

C7

C–E–G–B♭

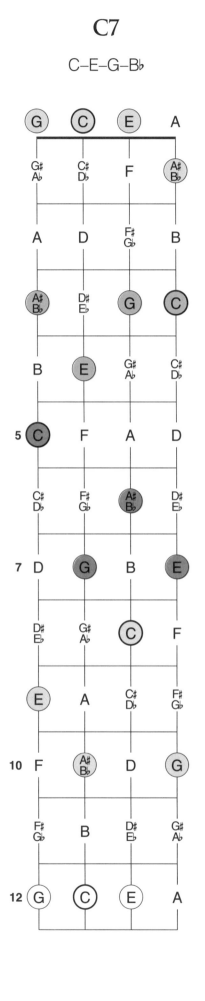

C♯/D♭7

C♯–E♯–G♯–B/D♭–F–A♭–C♭

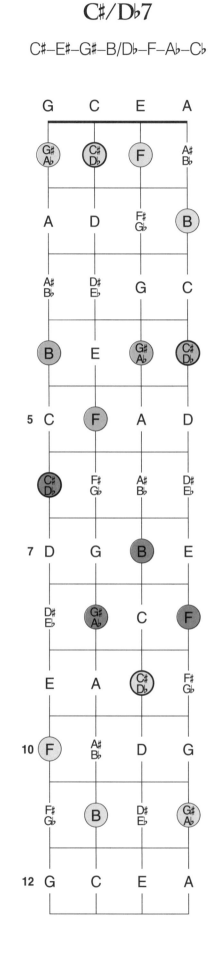

D7

D–F♯–A–C

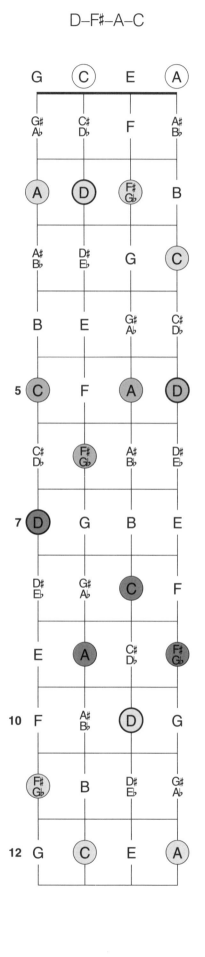

E♭7

E♭–G–B♭–D♭

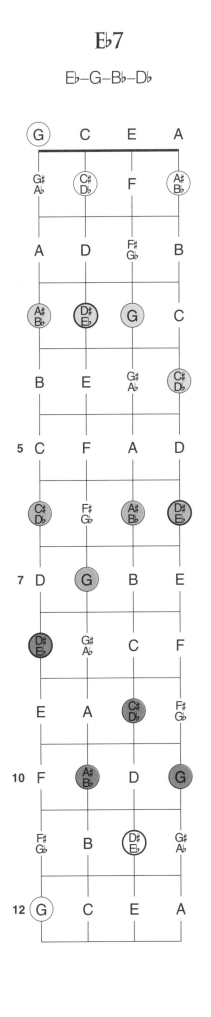

E7

E–G#–B–D

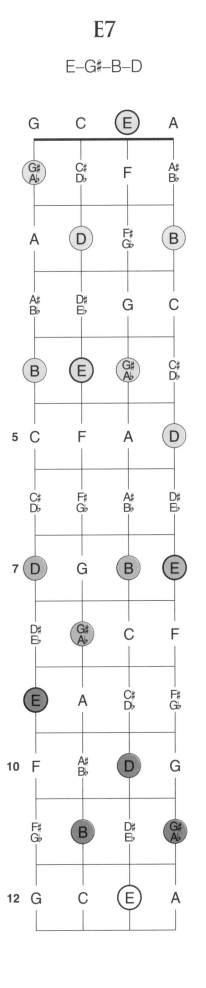

F7

F–A–C–E♭

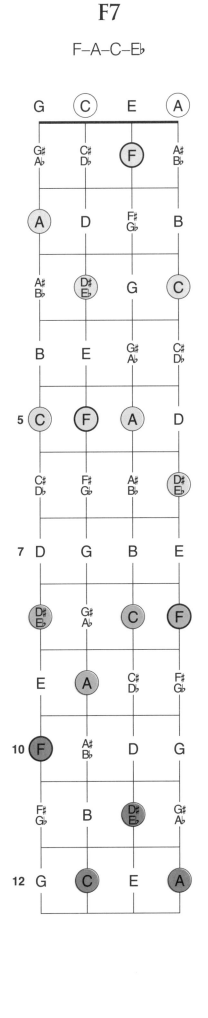

F♯/G♭7

F♯–A♯–C♯–E/G♭–B♭–D♭–F♭

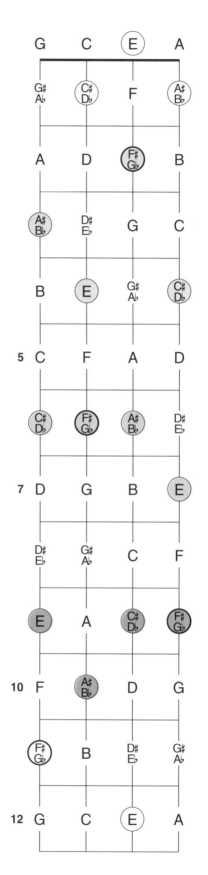

G7

G–B–D–F

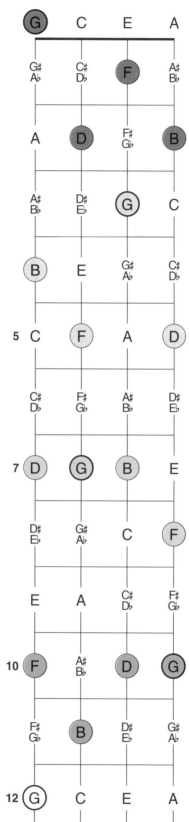

A♭7

A♭–C–E♭–G♭

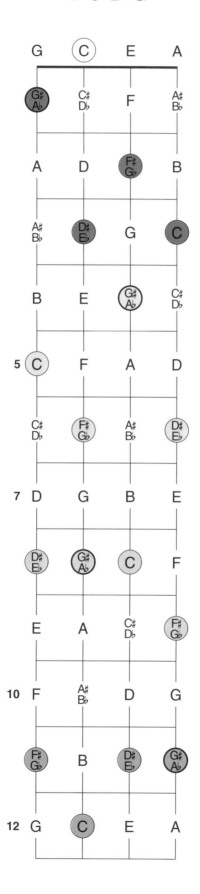

A7

A–C#–E–G

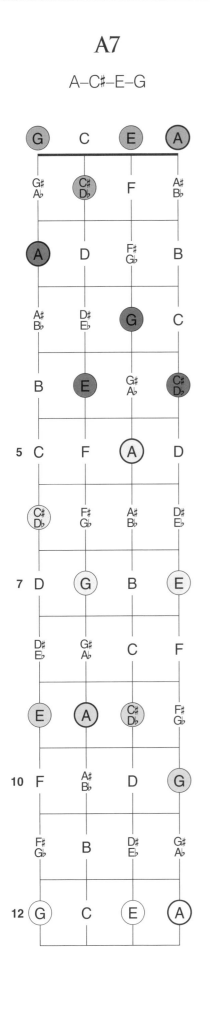

B♭7

B♭–D–F–A♭

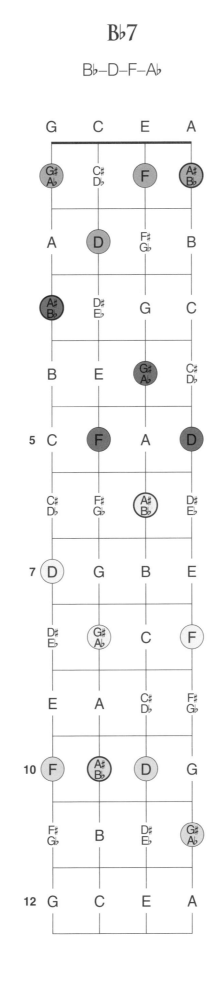

B7

B–D#–F#–A

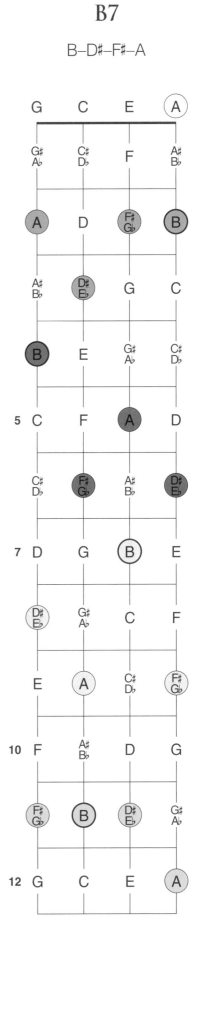

C7sus4

C–F–G–B♭

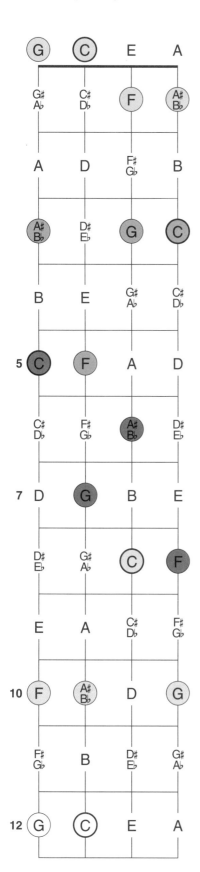

C♯/D♭7sus4

C♯–F♯–G♯–B/D♭–G♭–A♭–C♭

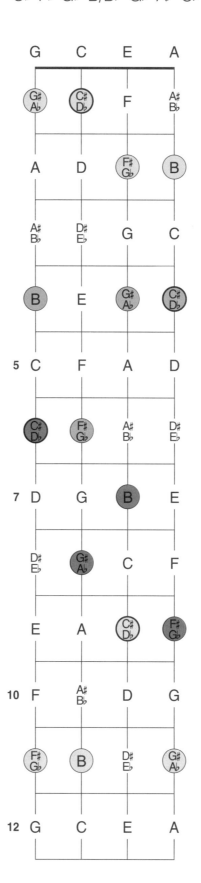

D7sus4

D–G–A–C

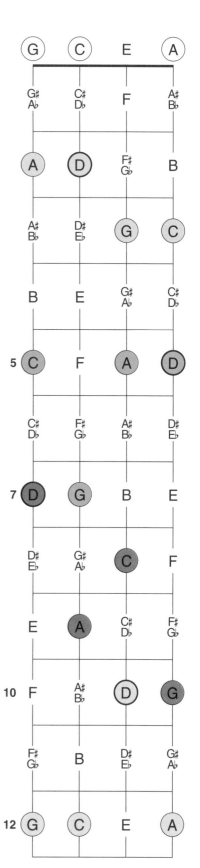

E♭7sus4

E♭–A♭–B♭–D♭

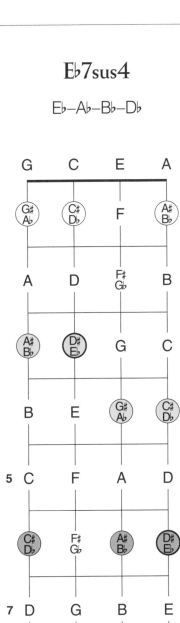

E7sus4

E–A–B–D

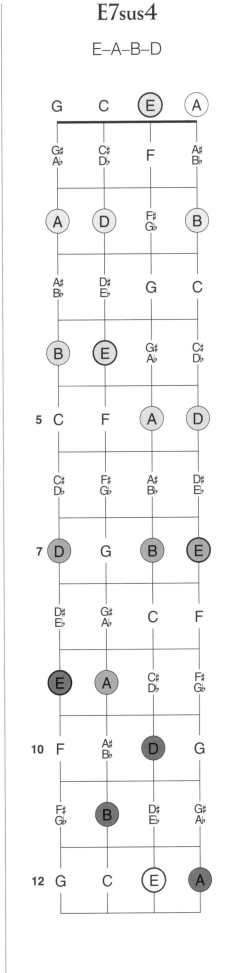

F7sus4

F–B♭–C–E♭

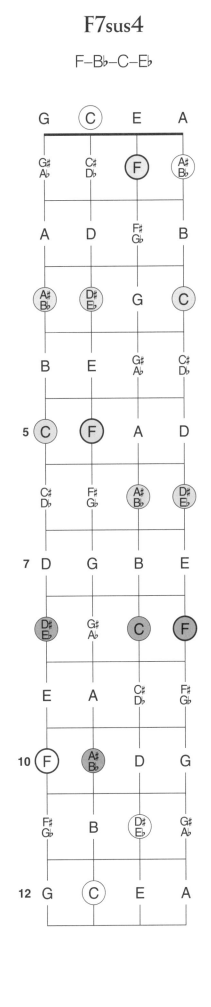

F♯7sus4

F♯–B–C♯–E

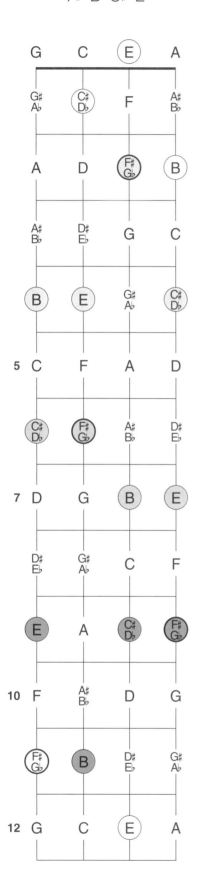

G7sus4

G–C–D–F

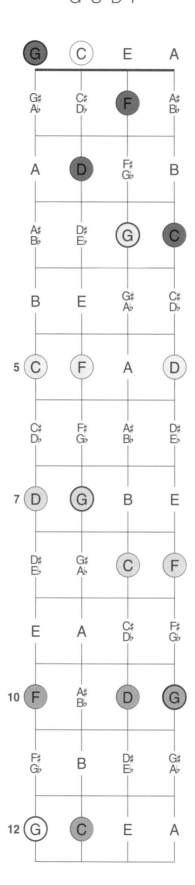

A♭7sus4

A♭–D♭–E♭–G♭

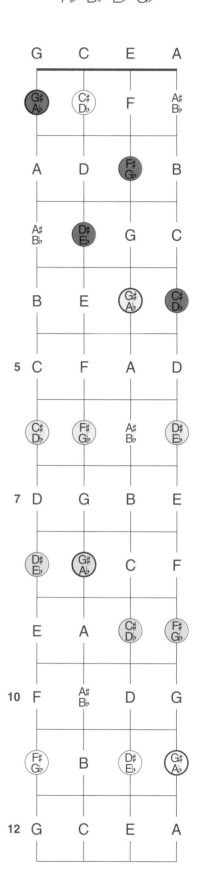

A7sus4

A–D–E–G

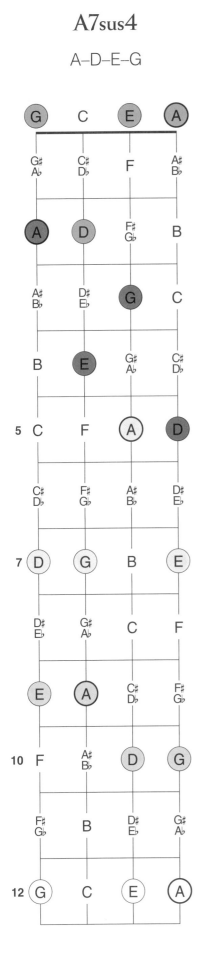

B♭7sus4

B♭–E♭–F–A♭

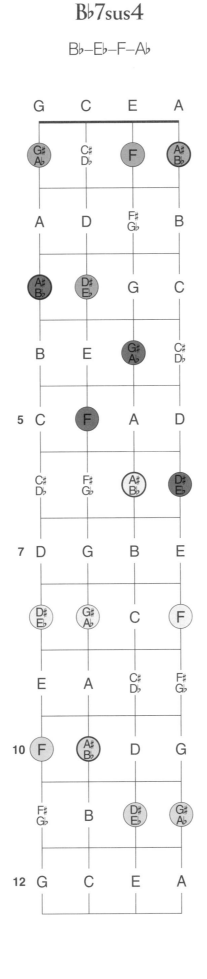

B7sus4

B–E–F#–A

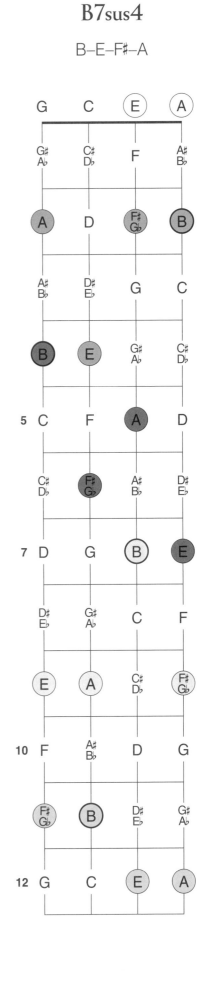

Cm7

C–Eb–G–Bb

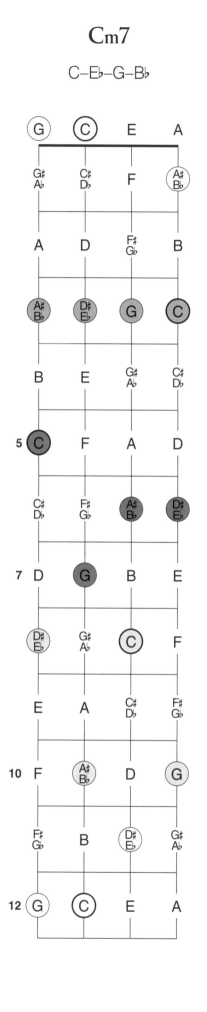

C#m7

C#–E–G#–B

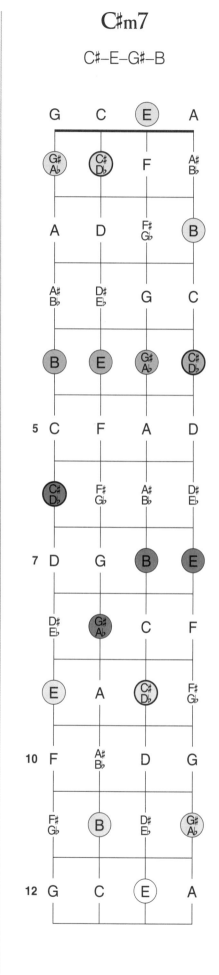

Dm7

D–F–A–C

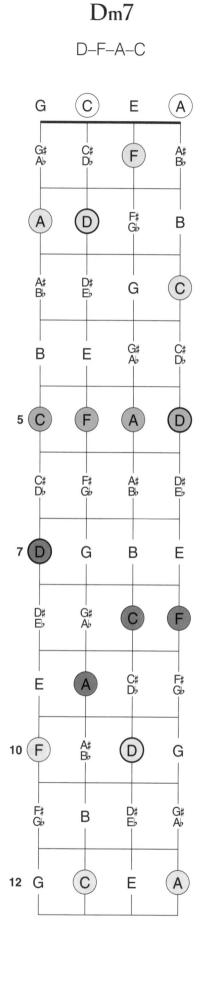

Ebm7

Eb–Gb–Bb–Db

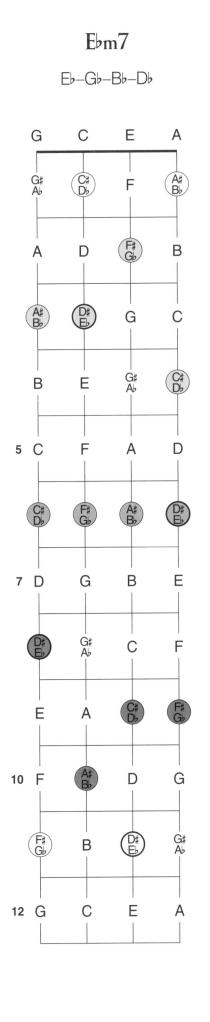

Em7

E–G–B–D

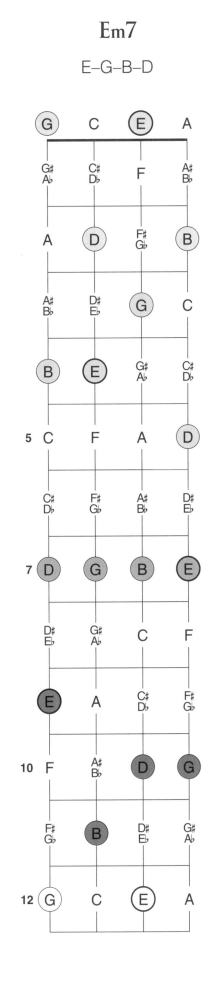

Fm7

F–Ab–C–Eb

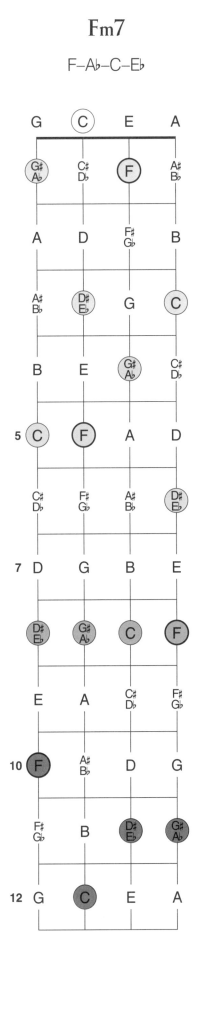

F#m7

F#–A–C#–E

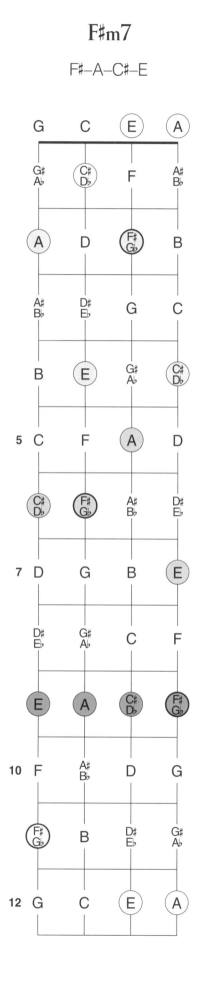

Gm7

G–B♭–D–F

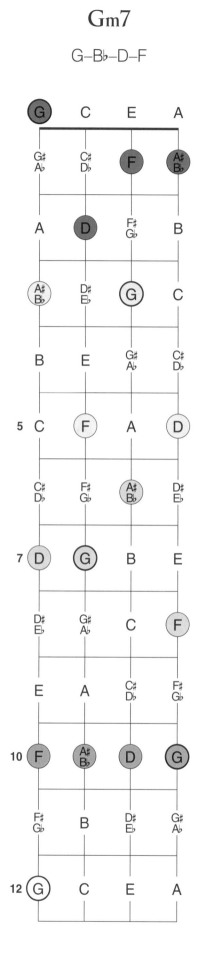

A♭m7

A♭–C♭–E♭–G♭

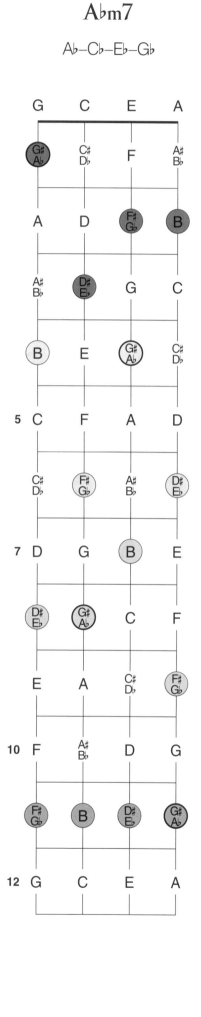

Am7

A–C–E–G

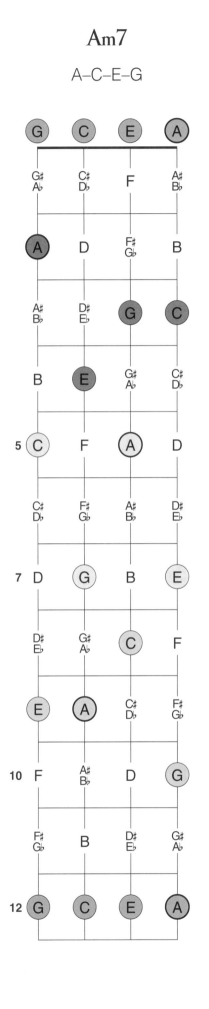

B♭m7

B♭–D♭–F–A♭

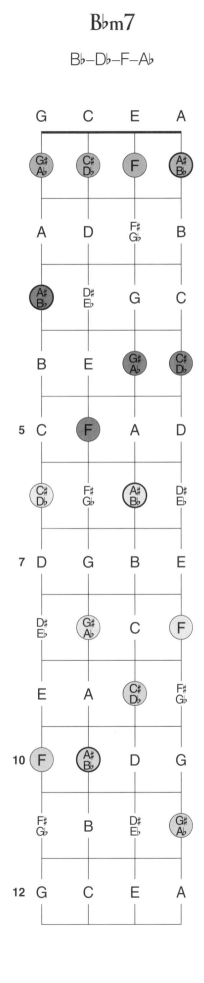

Bm7

B–D–F#–A

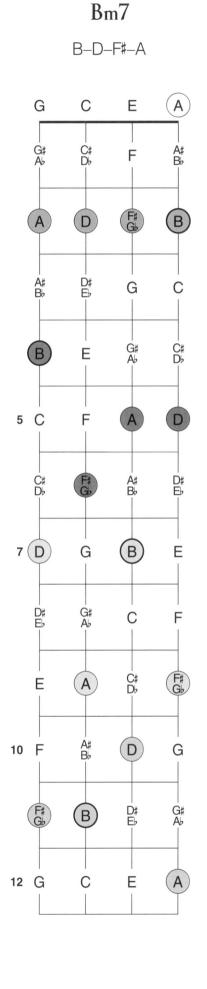

Cm(maj7)

C–E♭–G–B

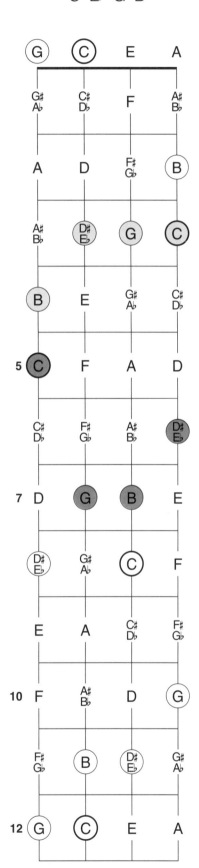

C♯m(maj7)

C♯–E–G♯–B♯

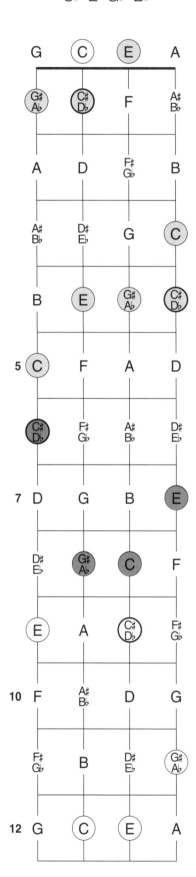

Dm(maj7)

D–F–A–C♯

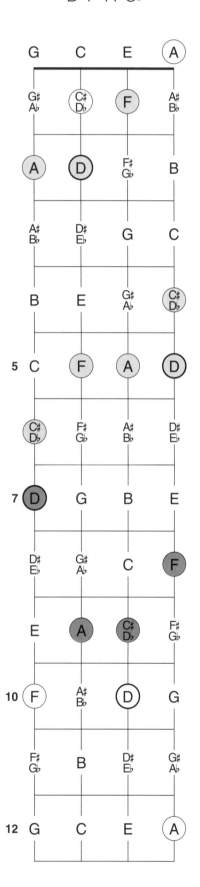

E♭m(maj7)

E♭–G♭–B♭–D

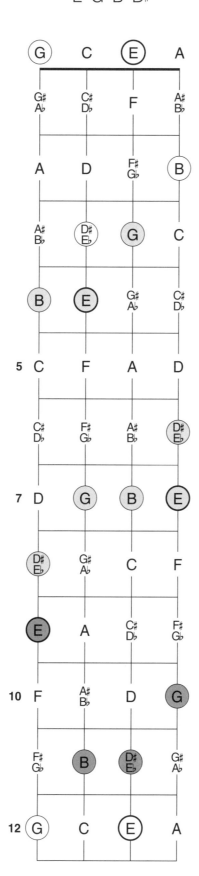

Em(maj7)

E–G–B–D♯

Fm(maj7)

F–A♭–C–E

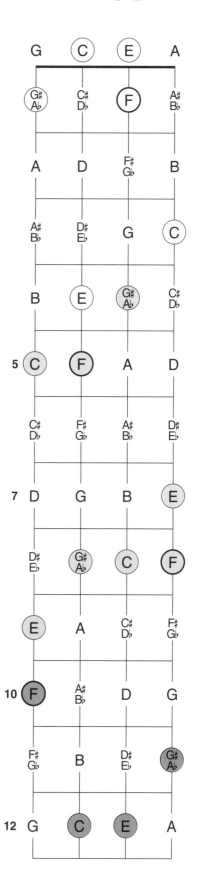

F#m(maj7)

F#–A–C#–E#

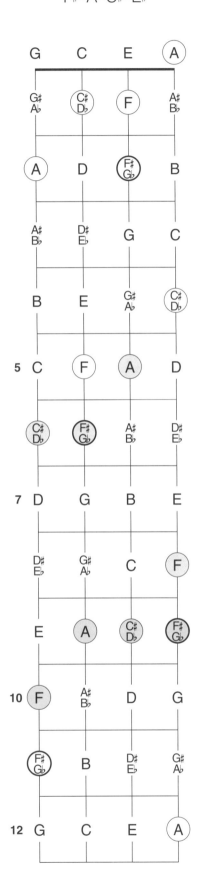

Gm(maj7)

G–B♭–D–F#

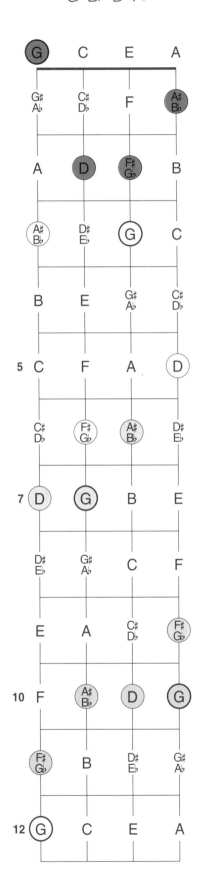

A♭m(maj7)

A♭–C♭–E♭–G

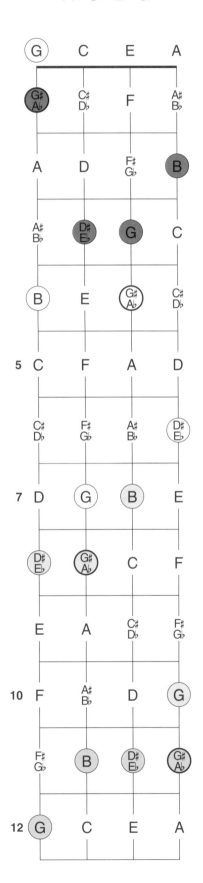

Am(maj7)

A–C–E–G♯

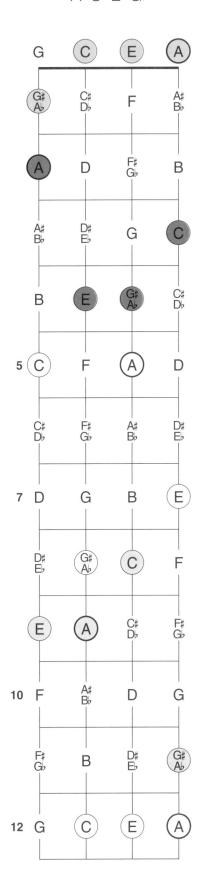

B♭m(maj7)

B♭–D♭–F–A

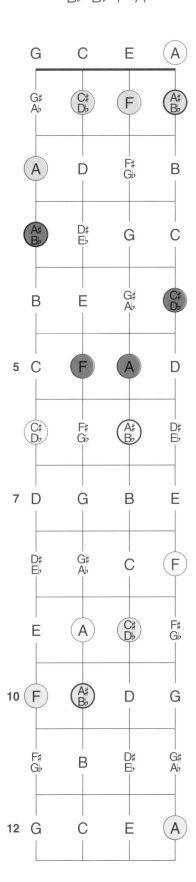

Bm(maj7)

B–D–F♯–A♯

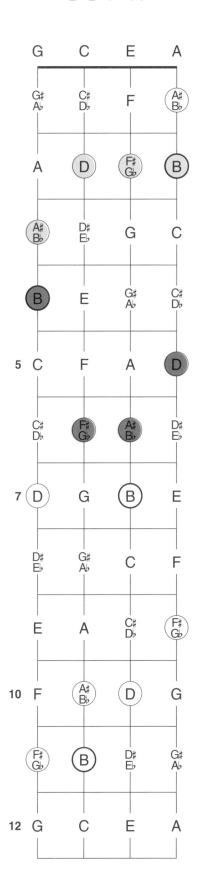

Cm7♭5

C–E♭–G♭–B♭

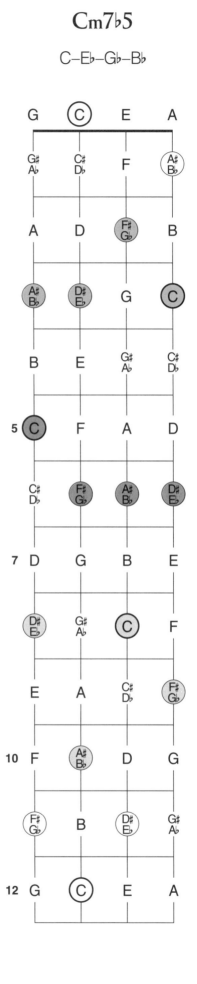

C#m7♭5

C#–E–G–B

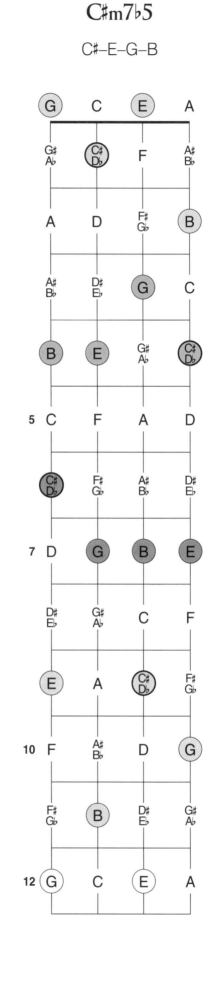

Dm7♭5

D–F–A♭–C

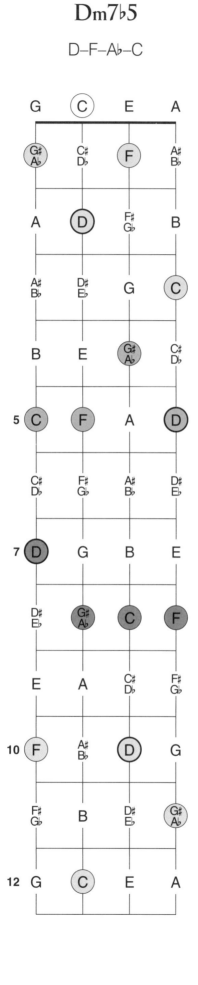

Ebm7b5

Eb–Gb–Bbb–Db

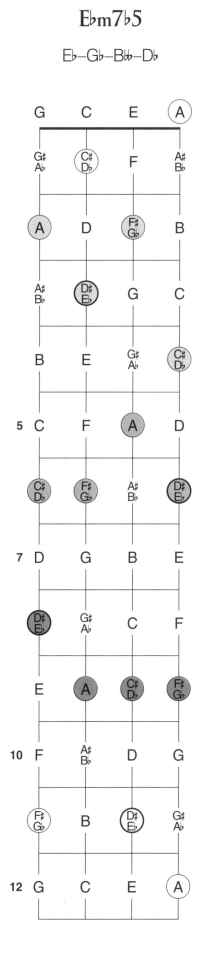

Em7b5

E–G–Bb–D

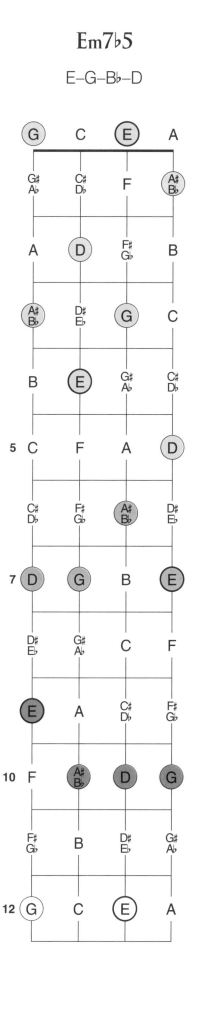

Fm7b5

F–Ab–Cb–Eb

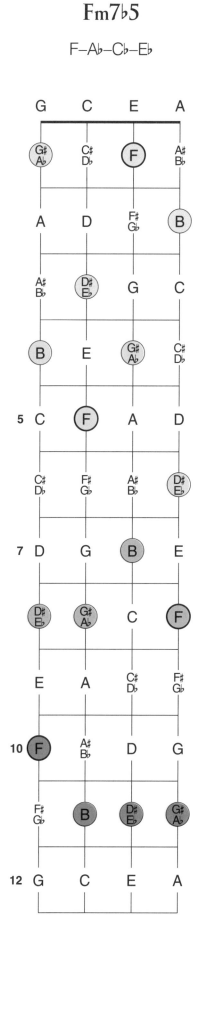

F#m7♭5

F#–A–C–E

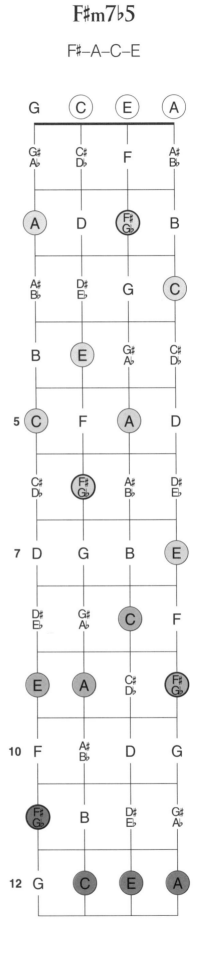

Gm7♭5

G–B♭–D♭–F

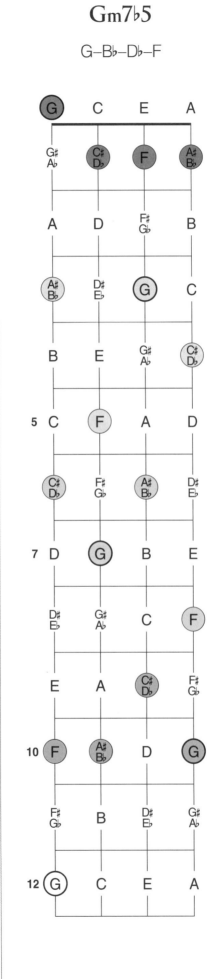

G#m7♭5

G#–B–D–F#

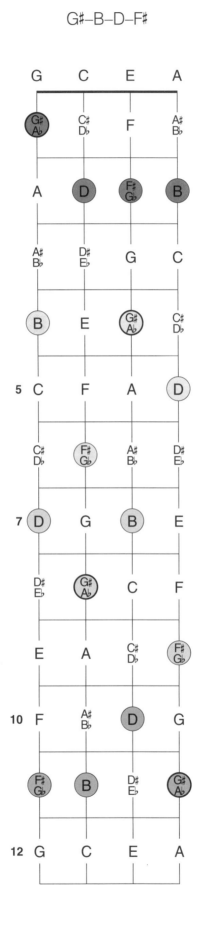

Am7♭5

A–C–E♭–G

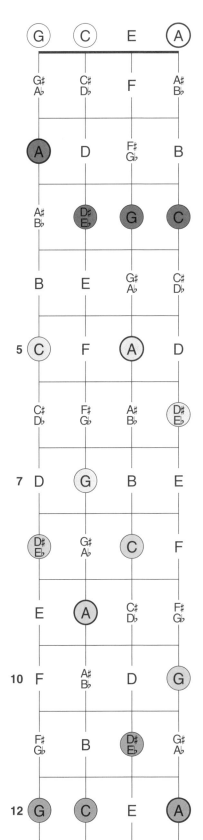

B♭m7♭5

B♭–D♭–F♭–A♭

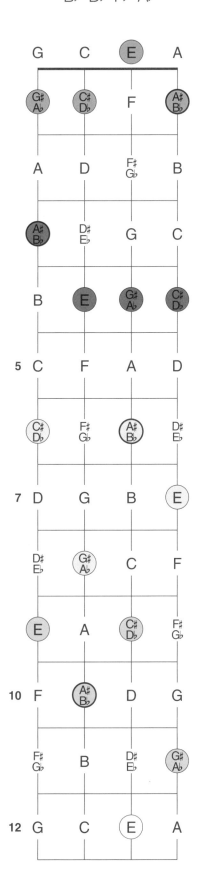

Bm7♭5

B–D–F–A

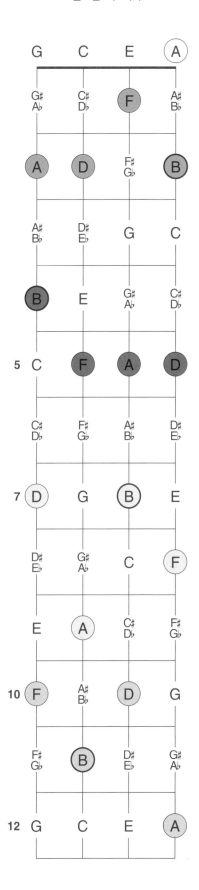

C°7

C–E♭–G♭–A

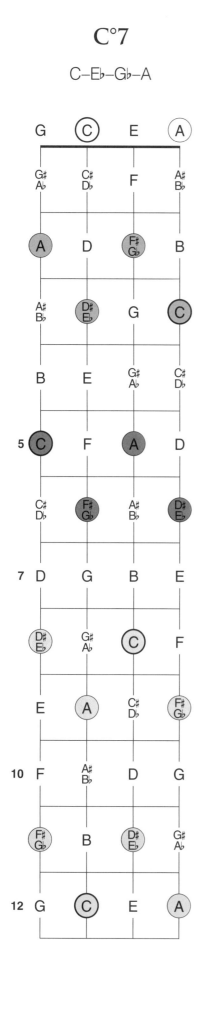

C♯°7

C♯–E–G–B♭

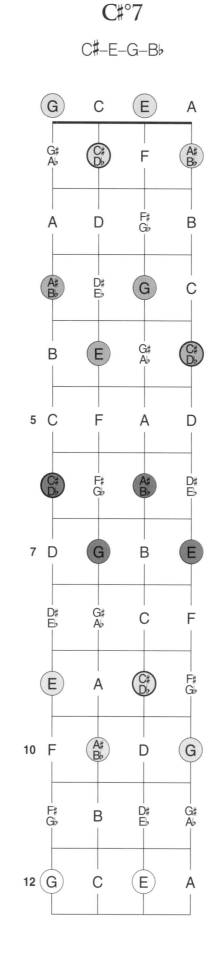

D°7

D–F–A♭–C♭

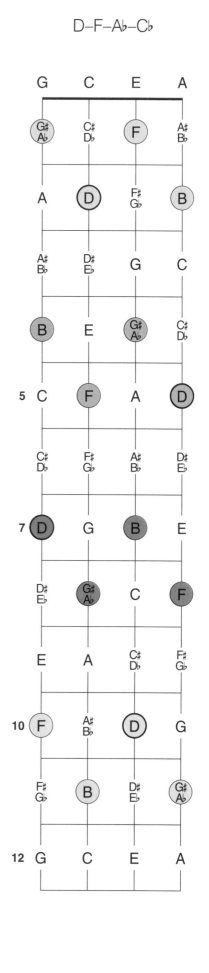

D#°7

D#–F#–A–C

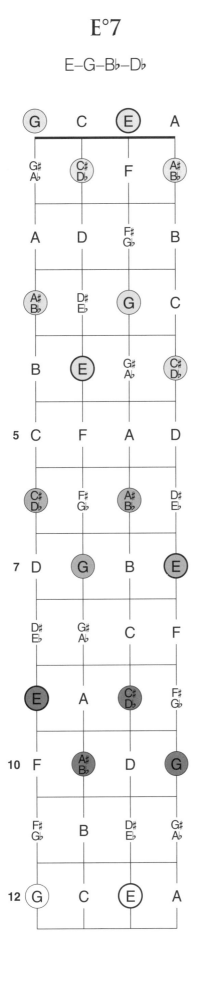

E°7

E–G–B♭–D♭

F°7

F–A♭–C♭–D

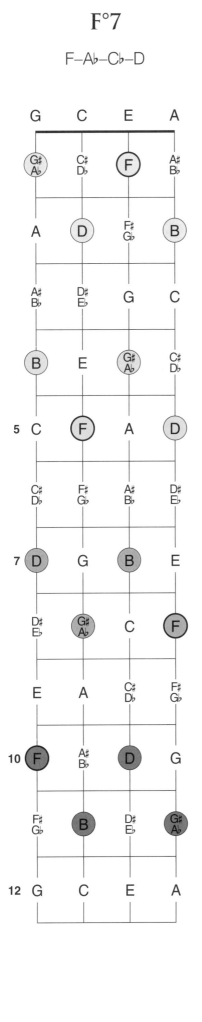

F#°7

F#–A–C–E♭

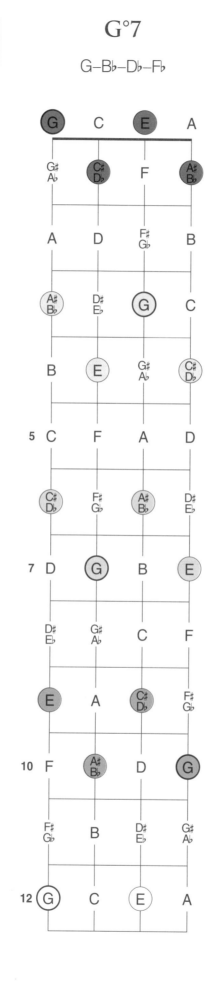

G°7

G–B♭–D♭–F♭

G#°7

G#–B–D–F

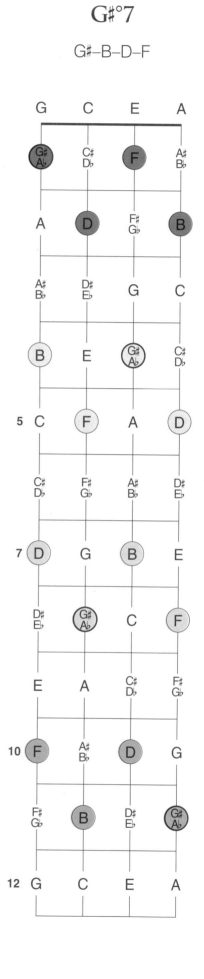

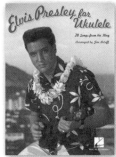

UKULELE ENSEMBLE SERIES

The songs in these collections are playable by any combination of ukuleles (soprano, concert, tenor or baritone). Each arrangement features the melody, a harmony part, and a "bass" line. Chord symbols are also provided if you wish to add a rhythm part. For groups with more than three or four ukuleles, the parts may be doubled.

CHRISTMAS CAROLS
Early Intermediate Level
Away in a Manger • Carol of the Bells • Deck the Hall • The First Noel • God Rest Ye Merry, Gentlemen • Hark! the Herald Angels Sing • It Came Upon the Midnight Clear • Jingle Bells • Joy to the World • O Christmas Tree • O Come, All Ye Faithful • O Holy Night • O Little Town of Bethlehem • Silent Night • Up on the Housetop.
00129248 .... $9.99

CHRISTMAS SONGS
Early Intermediate Level
The Chipmunk Song • The Christmas Song (Chestnuts Roasting on an Open Fire) • Do You Hear What I Hear • Feliz Navidad • Frosty the Snow Man • Have Yourself a Merry Little Christmas • Here Comes Santa Claus (Right Down Santa Claus Lane) • A Holly Jolly Christmas • (There's No Place Like) Home for the Holidays • Jingle Bell Rock • The Little Drummer Boy • Merry Christmas, Darling • The Most Wonderful Time of the Year • Silver Bells • White Christmas.
00129247 .... $9.99

CLASSIC ROCK
Mid-Intermediate Level
Aqualung • Behind Blue Eyes • Born to Be Wild • Crazy Train • Fly Like an Eagle • Free Bird • Hey Jude • Low Rider • Moondance • Oye Como Va • Proud Mary • (I Can't Get No) Satisfaction • Smoke on the Water • Summertime Blues • Sunshine of Your Love.
00103904 .... $9.99

HAWAIIAN SONGS
Mid-Intermediate Level
Aloha Oe • Beyond the Rainbow • Harbor Lights • Hawaiian War Chant (Ta-Hu-Wa-Hu-Wai) • The Hawaiian Wedding Song (Ke Kali Nei Au) • Ka-lu-a • Lovely Hula Hands • Mele Kalikimaka • The Moon of Manakoora • One Paddle, Two Paddle • Pearly Shells (Pupu 'O 'Ewa) • Red Sails in the Sunset • Sleepy Lagoon • Song of the Islands • Tiny Bubbles.
00119254 .... $9.99

THE NUTCRACKER
Late Intermediate Level
Arabian Dance ("Coffee") • Chinese Dance ("Tea") • Dance of the Reed-Flutes • Dance of the Sugar Plum Fairy • March • Overture • Russian Dance ("Trepak") • Waltz of the Flowers.
00119908 .... $9.99

ROCK INSTRUMENTALS
Late Intermediate Level
Beck's Bolero • Cissy Strut • Europa (Earth's Cry Heaven's Smile) • Frankenstein • Green Onions • Jessica • Misirlou • Perfidia • Pick Up the Pieces • Pipeline • Rebel 'Rouser • Sleepwalk • Tequila • Walk Don't Run • Wipe Out.
00103909 .... $9.99

STANDARDS & GEMS
Mid-Intermediate Level
Autumn Leaves • Cheek to Cheek • Easy to Love • Fly Me to the Moon • I Only Have Eyes for You • It Had to Be You • Laura • Mack the Knife • My Funny Valentine • Theme from "New York, New York" • Over the Rainbow • Satin Doll • Some Day My Prince Will Come • Summertime • The Way You Look Tonight.
00103898 .... $9.99

THEME MUSIC
Mid-Intermediate Level
Batman Theme • Theme from E.T. (The Extra-Terrestrial) • Forrest Gump – Main Title (Feather Theme) • The Godfather (Love Theme) • Hawaii Five-O Theme • He's a Pirate • Linus and Lucy • Mission: Impossible Theme • Peter Gunn • The Pink Panther • Raiders March • (Ghost) Riders in the Sky (A Cowboy Legend) • Theme from Spider Man • Theme from "Star Trek®" • Theme from "Superman."
00103903 .... $9.99

HAL•LEONARD®
CORPORATION
7777 W. BLUEMOUND RD. P.O. BOX 13819 MILWAUKEE, WI 53213

www.halleonard.com

A°7

A–C–E♭–G♭

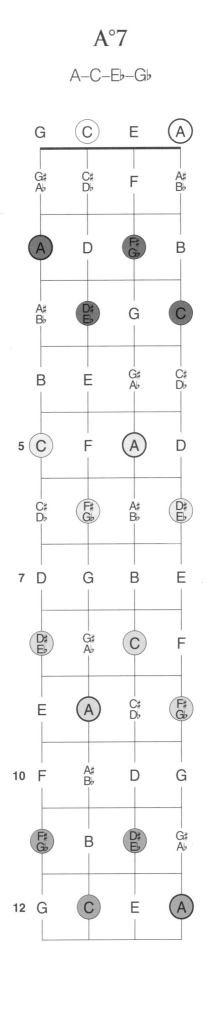

B♭°7

B♭–D♭–F♭–G

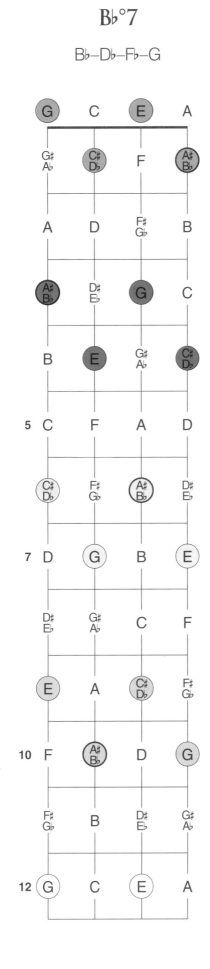

B°7

B–D–F–A♭

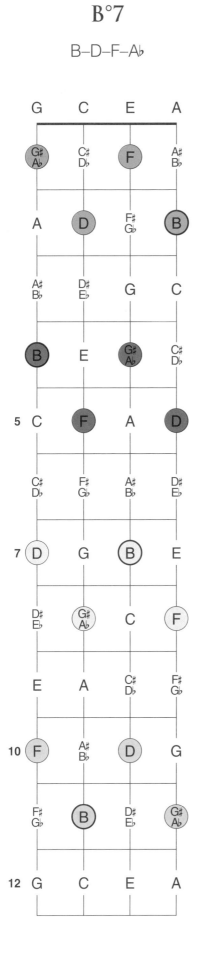

HAL·LEONARD® UKULELE PLAY-ALONG

AUDIO ACCESS INCLUDED

HAL·LEONARD®

www.halleonard.com

0517